A CLOSER LOOK AT NEW AGE SPIRITUALITY

By the same author

A CLOSER LOOK AT
New Age Spirituality

ROB FROST

KINGSWAY PUBLICATIONS
EASTBOURNE

ISBN 1 84291 006 X

Published by
KINGSWAY COMMUNICATIONS LTD
Lottbridge Drove, Eastbourne, BN23 6NT, England.
Email: books@kingsway.co.uk

Book design and production for the publishers by
Bookprint Creative Services, P.O. Box 827, BN21 3YJ, England.
Printed in Great Britain.

Thanks and Dedication

With thanks to David Hull for his research, to Meryl Smith
for compiling the manuscript, and to my publishers for
their constant encouragement. Special thanks to the New
Age Spirituality Concept Group, who have been looking at
these issues with me in recent months.

I dedicate this book to all my friends in the New Age
movement who are fellow travellers. May they discover
the One who is the source of all things.

Contents

1

Towards the New Age

For too long the church has seen the New Age movement as a threat, an enemy, and a source of evil in the world. I began to write this book as a diatribe of Bible verses and theology condemning it.

I repent.

Since meeting some of those involved in New Age activity, hanging around their bookshops and fairs and hearing them talk of their genuine quest for reality, I've changed my perspective. Now, I'm asking: what can I learn from the emerging New Age spirituality? What can it teach me? How can it help me?

To be frank, I am deeply disillusioned with what the church is offering Sunday by Sunday. There is a deadness in the ritual, a dryness in the formality, and a growing irrelevance in the institution. At least I find a genuine hunger for spiritual things in the New Age community, an openness to try new ideas, and a deep respect for the beliefs of others.

I expect that some of my more conservative Christian friends will be going through this manuscript with a fine toothcomb to weigh its theological accuracy, and to see if the author has lost his 'evangelical marbles'. They will interpret my reference to 'becoming a New Age Christian' as an indication that this book is not authentically Christian, or that I'm somehow allowing the New Age to write my personal agenda instead of the living Christ.

Well, I have an empty file ready and waiting for their hate mail! Those who respond thus, however, will have missed the point of the whole exercise. What I've discovered in the years of study behind this book is deeply significant for the contemporary Christian church. If I've missed some fine nuance of Christian believing, please forgive me, but my message is that the New Age movement is God's biggest 'wake-up call' to the church for centuries! If we miss it, and turn back to the slumbering yawn of much contemporary churchianity, then we've lost the plot.

The shape of the future church must be moulded to fit the New Age culture in which we find ourselves. If we, the followers of Jesus, are to be relevant to the felt needs of the people around us, we must become more spiritual. We must hear what God is saying through the hunger for spirituality that meets us on every side.

The enculturalisation of Christianity isn't primarily about the look of our buildings or the shape of our liturgy. It's about us, the kingdom people. It's about our spirituality. It's about whether we are truly alive to the realm of the Spirit. It's about 'being' rather than 'doing'. It's about a spiritual way of living. It's about a hunger for God-reality which will convince our neighbours that we really do believe.

Becoming a New Age Christian is not about a sell-out to New Age principles or practices. It's about discovering the kind of Christianity which Jesus modelled and which he spoke about when he said: 'I tell you the truth, no-one can enter the kingdom of God unless he is born of water and the Spirit. Flesh gives birth to flesh, but the Spirit gives birth to spirit' (John 3:5).

As a committed Christian with more than 30 years of valued Jesus-centred experience behind me, I openly admit that I am still searching. I am looking, like countless thousands of my peers, for something more. I identify with what Professor John Drane of Aberdeen University calls the 'spiritual searchers' of this present generation.

In *The McDonaldization of the Church* Drane points out that these people 'are of particular relevance to the church's predicament – because they are the ones who, in previous generations, would have been keen movers and shakers in parish life. Many of them are still activists in community affairs, but no longer through the church.'[1]

These 'spiritual searchers' are now to be found exploring alternative spiritualities in the New Age movement. This pursuit was once regarded as an alternative fringe activity, but is now an emerging culture in its own right. I see no contradiction in the fact that I am committed to Jesus Christ and yet searching for more reality in my spiritual life. Maybe I am becoming, then, a New Age Christian.

'New Age', of course, is an umbrella term and it refers to a galaxy of different activities, including health and well-being, therapy or self-help, the practice of an esoteric or spiritual tradition, concern for the environment and green issues, and respect for nature and feminine wisdom.

The roots of this movement go back to ancient times. They originate in Ancient Egypt and the India of the Vedas. This school of hermetic thought survived with the gnostics, the alchemists and the Qabalists, and resurfaced in the Renaissance.

The ancient practices of this spiritual quest were carried forward by people like Jacob Boehme in the sixteenth century, Emmanuel Swedenborg in the seventeenth and William Blake in the eighteenth. In the latter part of the nineteenth century there was a revival of occult activity, and with this came the public demonstrations of the Fox sisters in New York and the emergence of the modern spiritualist movement.

In 1875 the Theosophical Society was formed, which opened up the West to the mysterious doctrines of India. This was accompanied by an increasing interest in Freemasonry, with many new lodges being founded after 1860.

The current New Age movement was ushered into our hi-tech world by the Flower Power drug culture of the 1960s and 70s. Meditation techniques were learned from Eastern teachers like the Zen monk Shunryu Suzuki and the Maharishi from India who became popular icons in the West. Eileen Campbell, writing in *The Aquarian Guide to the New Age*, summed up the movement as

> a different perspective on life, one that is holistic, focusing on body, mind and spirit. At the heart of New Age thought is the idea that human beings have many levels of consciousness. In order to go about our business in the world we tend to function at the lower levels of consciousness . . . Fundamental to New Age belief is the idea that the awakening of the Higher Self is the goal of human life and that process of awakening is transformation. New Age techniques and methods help in the transformative process and the expansion of consciousness.[2]

While I struggle to understand or accept much of the heritage of the New Age movement, I can readily identify with the deep spiritual restlessness which is at the heart of it all. For that deep restlessness is at the heart of me. I want to readily admit that, after more than 25 years of Christian ministry, I'm convinced there is much more to the spiritual life than I've yet discovered, and I'm hungry for more!

I have a disturbing feeling that I've been scratching away at the surface of Christian spirituality, but have yet to discover what God has prepared for me. I've started on a journey but have yet to enter into the deep and mysterious places that the Lord would lead me into further down the track.

During the writing of this book I've been making a personal journey and asking painful questions about my own spirituality. For, ultimately, I share the hunger for the fulfilling kind of spirituality which is driving this New Age movement into the mainstream of our culture.

This book, then, is a record of my exploration of New Age thinking, and of my personal journey towards becoming a 'New Age Christian'. I invite you to join me as I wander around the supermarket of ideas of New Age culture, and see what they can teach me about my own quest for deeper spirituality.

I recognised that my starting point for such a journey must be a genuine hunger for spirituality. But what is spirituality? And how could I begin to define it? The British Government's Department for Education and Employment defines spirituality as 'the valuing of the non-material aspects of life, and intimations of an enduring reality'. W. H. Clark, however, writing in *The Psychology of Religion*, described it as 'the inner experience of the individual when he senses a Beyond, especially as evidenced by the effect of this experience on his behaviour when he actively attempts to harmonize his life with the Beyond'.[3]

I find no contradiction between the underlying hunger that leads someone to explore this kind of spirituality, and the hunger which drives me to know God better. We are both 'valuing the non-material aspects of life' and both 'sensing a Beyond'.

The first assumption of mysticism is that the soul is as real as any other organ of the body and in its proper sphere controls our spiritual welfare, allowing us to discern spiritual truth. I have no problem with that either, because the goal of Christian mysticism is to forge a 'profoundly personal relationship with the Creator; to experience, through contemplation, the very Presence of an individual God'.[4]

There is a long history of such mysticism within Christianity, and the vast breadth of literature on the subject is simply overwhelming. I began with the writings of the scholastic theologian Richard of St Victor (twelfth century) which seemed particularly appropriate to my search. He was the first known author to give a systematic account of mystical theology. In his short treatise 'Of the Four Degrees of Passionate Charity' he says:

> The third degree of love is when the mind of man is ravished into the abyss of divine light, so that the soul, having forgotten all outward things, is altogether unaware of itself, and passes out completely into its God.

This is what I'm looking for. For me, this is what it means to become a New Age Christian.

NOTES

1. John Drane, *The McDonaldization of the Church*, Darton, Longman and Todd 2000.
2. Eileen Campbell and J. H. Brennan, *The Aquarian Guide to the New Age*, Aquarian Press (Thorsons) 1990.
3. W. H. Clark, *The Psychology of Religion*, Macmillan 1958, p. 22.
4. O. B. Duane, *The Origins of Wisdom: Mysticism*, Brockhampton Press (Hodder Headline) 1997.

2

Towards a Richer Spirituality

My search to become a New Age Christian took me first to one of the largest New Age communities in Europe. As I climbed the rugged mud track, I had no idea what lay ahead, but I was very apprehensive. I had heard a lot about the community that lived there, and was full of ideas about what it might be like.

I met people who were eager to talk and to share. I spent several hours drinking warm sweet tea and chatting to a group of travellers, gathered under a tarpaulin roof. We were all sheltering from the dripping rain.

Philosophy was an integral part of their conversation, and the more I listened, the more impressed I became. These were not uneducated 'travellers'. Many of them were well read and university-trained, and most came from middle-class suburbia. They were thinkers. Their conversation resonated with a raw spirituality that I have rarely encountered in young people inside the church.

They spoke freely about mother earth, their connection with the seasons, their concern for the planet, the wonder of life itself, the importance of childbearing and the power of community. We talked freely about God, spirituality and eternity.

At that time in their rugged camp there was no running water, no electric power, no sanitation, no glitzy superstore . . . just a hunger for love, for spiritual reality and for a simpler perspective on life.

As I strode back down the muddy mountain track I wondered if they had recovered something which many of us have lost: an everyday spirituality; a sense of the divine; a piety not confined to religious buildings or sacred liturgies.

One of our mission teams established a Christian ministry among this large community of New Agers. From an initially hostile reception, the team created a well-respected Christian ministry of caring and service at the very centre of the community. We have all been deeply affected by it.

Our team's witness has largely been through practical acts of compassion, like play groups and youth clubs. Slowly the residents grew warmer towards the Christians among them and gradually became more open to talk about faith and spirituality. From the start the team spoke about Jesus and through love and care they earned the right to be heard.

What I saw in this community, however, resonated in my own life. They were looking for something more than the latest range of consumer durables. They were looking for ultimate reality. They had a lot to teach a New Age Christian like me.

The eminent sociologist Erich Fromm observed that such young people are by no means exceptional. They represent a growing quest for spirituality among the rising generation. He wrote:

> Quite against the expectations of their elders, who think their children have everything they wish, they rebel against the deadness and isolation of their lives. For the fact is – they do not have everything they wish for . . . and they wish for what they do not have.[1]

I have learnt from this New Age community that spiritual hunger cannot be satisfied by the latest techno toys, electronic devices, fashion garments or entertainment complexes. The deadness of such things has led these people, and thousands more beside, to leave them all behind in search of something more spiritually satisfying.

They are typical of 'Generation X' which represents those born in the 1960s and 70s. Not all of them opt for a primitive lifestyle on an Irish mountainside, but they are, nevertheless, deeply dissatisfied with their affluent lifestyle.

Kevin Ford, an observer of 'Generation X' culture, believes that they are looking for ways to escape the emptiness they feel. They are obsessed with leisure and yet timetabled to death. Loneliness scares them more than anything else, so they go flat out and live life at full throttle. They dread the day when they will run out of steam. Ford believes that the overscheduling and workaholism evident in this age group are symptoms of their need to escape. They just can't bear to be alone with time to reflect.[2]

The growing influence of 'rave' culture feeds the thinking and imagination of tens of thousands of these young people. It's a culture bound up with the use of the drugs LSD and Ecstasy, and it seeks to satisfy spiritual hunger.

Research carried out by the Home Office in their bi-annual British Crime Survey took a representative sample of 10,000 people in England and Wales. The authors concluded that there must be 121,000 regular users of the drug Ecstasy, while 728,000 more have tried it. They believe that there are even more users of LSD, with 152,000 regular users and 1,334,000 who have tried it.

After my teenage son went to a rave disco he introduced me to a group of 'ravers', whose story fascinated me. I persuaded them to join me for a live radio discussion with members of the drugs squad and several anti-drugs campaigners.

What amazed all of us taking part in the broadcast was that the reasons they gave for using drugs were more about a search for spirituality than the need for a Friday night 'high'. What I had written off as just another teenage fad was, in fact, a hunger for spiritual reality.

The loud repetitive thump of the music, the panoply of lights and lasers, and the eerie drifting smoke are the backdrop to something much more interesting than a new kind of dance craze. Thousands of young people are using raves to explore the inner world. They are crying out to be spiritual. For some of them, raves are seen as spiritual experiences and 'ecstasy' as a communion with the supernatural.

Terence McKenna, author of *True Hallucinations*, views the rave as an explosive attempt to free consciousness from its unnatural ego-centred state. He believes our natural state has become regulated out of existence, except in a diluted form in churches, sports stadia and discotheques. McKenna writes:

What fascinates me is that the rave culture, seen as purely hedonistic by the establishment, is frequently regarded as a spiritual event by those involved. Raves are likened to trance-like tribal rituals where ravers celebrate their unity and shared uplifted state, giving and receiving from one another.

He is not alone in thinking this. Dr Russell Newcombe, a Liverpool-based sociologist and researcher, wrote the paper 'Raving and Dance Drugs'. He observed that raving can be viewed as a transcendental mind-altering experience providing psychic relief to 'alienated people in a secular repressive and materialistic society. Ecstasy and other drugs are the keys that unlock the doors to these desired states of consciousness.'

In a high-pressure world, where success is everything, many are looking for something more lasting. Nicholas Saunders of *The Guardian* surveyed 137 ravers about the effects of Ecstasy on their lives. A significant number reported 'increased spiritual awareness' – some adding that they 'felt closer to nature, calmer and more appreciative of life itself'.

I empathise with this quest for spiritual reality. It's something that I want more of, even though I am a committed Christian. I'm not alone! Tens of thousands of people in their twenties, thirties and forties are exploring a growing number of new forms of popular spirituality. This exploration is one of the most significant characteristics of postmodern society.

Hundreds of thousands of ordinary people continue their inward journey of discovery in weekly yoga classes, Tai Chi groups, meditation sessions, aromatherapy clinics, and occult covens in communities all over the country.

Recently I crossed the threshold of the New Age shop in a small Devon town. I hoped that none of my evangelical Christian friends would think I'd lost my senses as I browsed the bookshelves and eavesdropped the conversations by the health food display cabinet.

The people in the shop, which was one of several in the high street, were buying books on meditation, tapes for relaxation, and homeopathic and health-food products. Their search for spirituality had become part of the Saturday shopping ritual . . . sandwiched somewhere between Boots and Sainsbury's. The hunger for the spiritual has become a mainstream need.

Sadly, a casual interest in homeopathy can sometimes lead to something much more serious. Jane Newport, for example, felt that she had reached a time in her life when she needed 'to seek harmony with myself, make peace with my past and move forward, unfettered by past mistakes'. She was 42, and her husband had just left her. She was devastated. 'I left our busy town house, and the security of being married to a successful solicitor, and bought a small home in the country. Isolated from my friends I sought a new way of being. I wanted different values, new meanings, and solutions to the mysteries of my life.'

How I wish that Jane Newport's story told of some triumphant experience of Christ. But no, her 'testimony' appeared in a guide to natural therapies, and her journey took her into a Buddhist order, Tai Chi, and Shen. Her story is typical of many who have not found what they were looking for in the traditional forms of church life.

The New Age shop was one of the busiest shops in the high street, spiritual things were discussed freely there, and there was an openness to anyone seeking a spiritual perspective on life. I wondered if there was more talk of the spiritual disciplines here than in the church directly opposite. All it advertised was an autumn bazaar and a holiday slide show.

The search for meaning is on. The eminent psychologist C. J. Jung observed that among all his patients in the second half of life (those over 35) the problem of each one was the lack of a religious outlook on life. We disregard the spiritual side of our existence at our peril.

Sociologists tell us that the modernist era has ignored the spiritual dimension of our humanity in favour of scientific method. Postmodernity, however, reaffirms the importance of the mystical and the reality of the spiritual.

Leighton Ford traces this postmodern emphasis on the 'experiential' to Einstein.

> The massive shift . . . from modernism to postmodernism can be traced to the beginning of the twentieth century, when Einstein's theory of relativity overthrew the Enlightenment and spawned the physics of Isaac Newton. Einstein's theory upset all previous assumptions of the nature of reality. There is no such thing as an objective point of view in matters of physics; all viewpoints are relative in space and time. Under some conditions, subjective experience supersedes objective measurements . . . Subjective experience supersedes logic and objective facts.[3]

Although some scientists object strongly to this kind of inference, there can be little doubt that this is a popular perception of science today.

If modernism emphasised the importance of the individual and the power of competition, postmodernism seeks to reunify knowledge and to exalt the importance of community. It is essentially a search for spirituality.

In an excellent review of the current societal scene, the Henley Centre published *The Paradox of Prosperity*, a detailed research project sponsored by the Salvation Army.

This research concluded:

> There is a growing demand for some sort of alternative approach to life, for new answers to old questions. This has led to the emergence of a renewed emphasis on spirituality. There is recognition that true 'wealth' comes from spiritual as much as material sources, and people are drawing up an alternative scale of 'value' that will restore meaning to their lives. 27% of people claim to have successfully changed their spiritual life and a further 20% would like to do so. [4]

I identify with this 20% of the British population that want to change their spiritual life. I am part of this generation and am caught up in this cultural movement. I remain a committed Christian, but I want more!

I've become increasingly dissatisfied with the dry institutional deadness of much of what I see on offer in my local church each Sunday. And I've become more and more intolerant of the noisy unstructured mayhem which passes for worship in many 'renewed' churches.

I've been wondering if it's some kind of mid-life Christian crisis, or if it's something to do with my own development as a Christian. Strangely enough, however, the more I've mentioned it to my Christian friends the more concerned I've become. It seems that a lot of other Christians are feeling just the same.

Postmodernism is all about a rediscovery of roots, and this journey through the New Age movement has challenged me to rediscover the richness of my Christian heritage and to connect with the mystery of its ancient spiritual culture.

John Garvey notes:

It's hard to imagine the use of a word like spirituality by Maximus the Confessor or one of the Fathers or Mothers of the Desert, who didn't think that they were talking about a category called spirituality but rather about the way the souls of human beings work – about the most basic human truths.[5]

My research into Christian mysticism leads me to understand that I can only become a New Age Christian when I reorientate my life. My spirituality cannot be based on an hour in church on Sunday! It must develop through the whole of my being and in every aspect of my living.

'Everything you do or say, then,' wrote Paul, 'should be done in the name of the Lord Jesus, as you give thanks through him to God the Father' (Colossians 3:17 GNB).

The quality of my spirituality flows from the quality of my life. Spirituality is what I take to church, not what I go to enhance. Christian spirituality is about a 24/7 lifestyle of sacrifice, not a weekly opportunity to get blessed.

My contact with New Agers has convinced me that I need to rediscover the lost art of 'practising the presence of God'. I must find a new awareness of the holy and come to prayer with a new hunger for the 'God who is beyond'. I must learn how to pray with body, mind and spirit and to worship in a way that will renew and transform me. I must learn how to echo Paul's experience when he wrote: 'What should I do, then? I will pray with my spirit, but I will also pray with my mind' (1 Corinthians 14:15 GNB).

My journey through contemporary New Age spirituality has led me to understand that my Christian spirituality must spring from my innermost being. There is a constancy there which will not be hindered by personal circumstances, mood swings or spiritual lows. Christian spirituality isn't about being stimulated by the latest 'mood enhancing' praise tape – it's about the core of my being in relationship with the Person of Jesus Christ.

On my journey towards a New Age Christianity I have learnt that I must connect with God through tears of sadness and through the anguish of suffering. I must recognise that nothing need prevent me from giving my 'sacrifice of praise'.

I am learning, as a result of this New Age Christian journey, that the whole of my life is an act of worship, not just an hour on Sundays. I have moved beyond this great divide between sacred and secular, Sunday and Monday. I have arrived at a place where all that I am, all that I do, and all that I hope to be is my daily offering to God.

As a New Age Christian I practise the presence of God while shopping in the supermarket and driving on congested roads. My spirituality flows from good family relationships and from caring for awkward colleagues. My spiritual life comes out of the frustration of difficult work and the joy of a job well done. It celebrates the presence of God in the nitty-gritty of everyday routine.

I am a New Age Christian. My Christian spirituality is not about religion; it's about living life in real connection with the Living God himself.

NOTES

1. E. Fromm, *To Have or To Be?* Jonathan Cape, p. 103.
2. Kevin Ford, *Jesus for a New Generation*, Hodder and Stoughton 1996.
3. Leighton Ford, *The Power of Story*, NavPress 1994.
4. *The Paradox of Prosperity*, The Henley Centre/Salvation Army 1999, p. 40.
5. John Garvey, *Death of a Princess*, SilverFish 1998, p. 61.

3

Towards a Greater Sense of Wholeness

I stood in the waiting room of the homeopathist in a small Devon town and viewed the prospectus which described his work. The introduction made it clear that he was quite unable to treat any patient who was unwilling to view their illness from a holistic perspective.

The instructions to patients stated that only after a detailed interview reviewing the patient's state of body, mind and spirit could he begin to focus on the symptoms of their illness. His publicity declared that his treatment 'takes account of you as a person – your individual characteristics, emotionally as well as physically, before treatment can begin'.

This view of human illness stems from the work of Samuel Hahnemann in 1796. He was a German doctor who took this revolutionary new approach to the cure of the sick. Like Hippocrates two thousand years earlier, he believed that there were two ways of treating ill health. He called them the way of opposites and the way of similars. Some see his work as the source of contemporary holism.

This awareness of the connection between body, mind

and spirit has often been highlighted by Prince Charles, who has become an enthusiastic advocate of holism. In a major speech to 70 academics, businessmen and religious leaders at Wilton Park, the foreign office conference centre, he said:

> In my view a more holistic approach is needed now. Modern materialism, in my humble opinion, is unbalanced and increasingly damaging in its long-term consequences. Science has tried to assume a monopoly, even a tyranny, over our understanding. Religion and science have become separated. Science has attempted to take over the natural world from God; it has fragmented the cosmos and relegated the sacred to a secondary compartment of our understanding, divorced from practical day to day existence. We are only now beginning to gauge the results of this disastrous outlook.[1]

It's little wonder then that 'holistic' has become the trendy buzz-word in everything from social work to education. Even the British Army has announced a more holistic approach to its new recruits. Holistic medicine, however, has grabbed the most media attention.

Holistic patient care is an umbrella term for looking at the overall health and lifestyle profile of a patient. It treats specific ailments not as conditions to be alleviated but rather as symptoms of a more fundamental disease.

The first formal link between conventional and holistic medicine was established in 1989 between the Hammersmith Hospital and the Bristol Cancer Health Centre. Conventional therapy and holistic treatment (including a vegan diet, counselling, and complete relaxation) were combined. Many hospitals, general practitioners and health professionals now view holism as the only proper way to treat patients. They view the links between body, mind and spirit as so strong that it's impossible to treat one aspect of a human being without considering the others.

Prince Charles is enthusiastic about this view of human healing. His speech concluded that 'hospitals need to be conceived and, above all, designed to reflect wholeness of healing if they are to help the process of recovery in a more complete way'.

It's little wonder, therefore, that more and more doctors are recommending meditation, aromatherapy and 'spiritual healers' as part of their total health care package. They are increasingly concerned about the connection between body, mind and spirit in the work of healing.

John Drane observes that holism takes a completely different view of the human condition from the very mechanical way of treatment of traditional Western medicine. He writes:

> Common human experience shows that it is possible to have a perfect body and still be unhappy – or, conversely, to be physically disabled and yet personally fulfilled. Human happiness is much more than the sum of its parts, and seems to be located somewhere in the interplay between different aspects of the personality. Holistic medicine claims to be treating not merely sickness or disease, but the whole person – body, mind and spirit. This is why self-knowledge is pretty central to all New Age medicine – and why, in the final analysis, it almost always comes down to specifically religious or spiritual considerations.[2]

This holistic view of the human condition which is so popular with New Agers isn't inconsistent with Christian faith. Many Christians have already made an outstanding Christian response to this whole genre of holistic practice.

The Kairon Prison Ministry organisation, set up by ex-Watergate conspirator Chuck Colson, has started an experimental project in a 24-bed wing of the Verne Prison in Dorset. Inmates are invited to join an 18-week programme which starts with a 40-hour intensive meeting stretching over three days. Prisoners are offered the chance to reform by mentoring and 'changing life through a higher being than themselves'. The ministry group claims to have cut re-offending rates significantly among prisoners in 150 jails in the United States. One of their ministries includes the management of an entire prison in the Sao Paulo state in Brazil.

Dame Cicely Saunders made a profound contribution to the care of the dying through her pioneering work in the hospice movement. Her ideas were inextricably tied to her Christian faith. Dame Cicely trained as a nurse, an almoner and later as a doctor in order to discover the best kind of care for the dying. The nuns at St Joseph's Hospice inspired her with their compassion and prayerfulness. She took this experience and combined it with the technology of symptom control and pain relief. She wrote:

> We believed that in this response we would learn to be the instruments of His care for the suffering and bereaved, and show our patients and their families the care by deeds rather than words which would help them into a healing relationship.[3]

Professor Baroness McFarlane, one of our country's most eminent nurses, believes that we cannot separate spiritual needs from physical needs. She teaches that the nurse, by virtue of her or his relationship with the patient, can give spiritual care as part of care of the total person. It is primarily the entire person of the nurse, interacting with the entire person of the patient, in a caring relationship. Communicating identity with touch and moistening the lips of the dying can be spiritual acts.[4] Christian ministry like this must be grounded in the love of Christ. We can only seek to care for the whole needs of others when we have discovered that the power of Christ can meet our own.

Mother Teresa's work in the slums of Calcutta was holistic in its healing ministry. She taught that it was the ministry to the patient's body, mind and spirit which was all-important. It was a vision which flowed out of her faith in Christ and her relationship with God. A nurse called Fi Hibberts was tending a skeletal dying man late one night when Mother Teresa pushed her closer to the patient. As she gripped them together she whispered, 'Love until it hurts.' Mother Teresa once said:

Are we convinced of Christ's love for us and of our love for him? . . . This conviction is the rock on which holiness is built by serving Christ's poor . . . Our works of charity are only the fruit of God's love in us. That is why those who are most united with him love their neighbour most.[5]

Elizabeth Babbs has been a great help to me in the research for this book. A trained teacher at the height of her career, she was quite suddenly struck down by M.E., the chronic fatigue syndrome. It seemed that her job, her social life and her future were suddenly terminated. She began to look into New Age spirituality as a key to unlock whatever was damaging her as a whole person. As a part of this, she began to explore Christian meditation, and it was through this experience that she found the reality of the living Christ. In 1991 she was suddenly and powerfully healed, and now travels the country leading spirituality workshops and facilitating others to discover Christ's healing power within the connection of body, mind and spirit.[6]

In one of her meditations she writes:

Lord, You look beyond my failings and see my needs
You reach out to me
Clasping me victoriously.
You walk ahead of me through the pain
And stoop down to cover me.
And Lord, when I can walk no further
You carry me.

Lord, You found me at the lowest point in my life
Unable to go on
Unable to function.
You saw rejection as an open door
And walked with me unravelling this shroud of grief
Gently touching my heart
And releasing me from captivity.[7]

In my journey towards becoming a New Age Christian, I have discovered the importance of a healthy body, mind and spirit. All through my formative years as a Christian I can recall endless sermons about the 'soul' or the 'spirit', but none about the body or the mind. I have come to believe that it is only when my body, mind and spirit are submitted to Christ that I become a whole person.

I am convinced that holism is at the very core of authentic Christian experience. Saint Paul's letter to the Colossians concludes:

> Since, then, you have been raised with Christ, set your heart on things above, where Christ is seated at the right hand of God. Set your mind on things above, not on earthly things. For you died, and your life is now hidden with Christ in God. (Colossians 3:1–3)

If I am to be truly integrated as a human being, my body, mind and spirit must be brought into harmony with the living Christ. I am only truly integrated as a child of God when every aspect of my being is centred on him. When my heart is fully yielded to him, and my emotions are consecrated to him and my body is under his control, then I am truly made whole.

M. Scott Peck, writing in *The Road Less Travelled and Beyond*, concluded:

> As a self-designated Christian, I personally not only believe that there is a 'Higher Power' behind the visible order of things, but also that 'It' is not neutral – that 'It' actively wants us to be in harmony with 'It'.[8]

New Agers have a lot to teach us. For far too long Christians have been preoccupied with the soul. It's only when the living Christ infuses our bodies, minds and spirits that we experience the kind of holistic Christian experience which Jesus described as being 'born again'.

Ultimately, Christians find their full potential when they become fully integrated into the reality of the living God. John Habgood summed up what it means to be a New Age Christian in the closing words of his book *Being a Person*:

> Our identity, our continuity, our value, all that matters about us, are ultimately what they are as they are held in the mind of

God. This is why the most obvious and familiar description remains the best. We are made in the image of God, and that contains both an assertion and a promise. 'Beloved, we are God's children now; it does not yet appear what we shall be, but we know that when he appears we shall be like him, for we shall see him as he is' (1 John 3:2).[9]

NOTES

1. *The Times*, 14 December 1996.
2. John Drane, *What Is the New Age Still Saying to the Church?*, Marshall Pickering 1999, p. 138.
3. Cicely Saunders, 'In quest of the spiritual component of care for the terminally ill', Yale University Press 1986.
4. J. McFarlane, *Spiritual Care*, Contact Publishing, p. 181.
5. Mother Teresa in G. Goree and J. Barbier (eds), *The Love of Christ*, Fount 1982.
6. Elizabeth Babbs, *Can God Help M.E.?* Eagle 1999.
7. Elizabeth Babbs, *Out of the Depths*, Eagle 2001, p.39.
8. M. Scott Peck, *The Road Less Travelled and Beyond*, Rider, p. 247.
9. John Habgood, *Being a Person*, Hodder and Stoughton 1998, p. 297.

4

Towards a Healing Touch

As part of my pilgrimage towards becoming a New Age Christian, I went to Totnes in Devon to see what range of healing activities were on offer. I was amazed at the diversity of options.

Marion Badenoch, PhD, a psychologist, was offering 'psychosynthesis therapy'. Her sessions recognise 'not just the power of the past in moulding our lives but also the role of our own potentials and the importance of innate "higher" values, like truth, compassion and joy in this process'.

The three-year course provided by the Devon School of Shiatsu gives students an experience of a healing art based on 'an understanding of the human body as a system of energy which circulates in channels called meridians'. Its exponents claim that it can be a 'profound means of self development'. Shiatsu is a very ancient form of healing practice which originated in China, but which is increasingly popular on the New Age scene today. It is basically a form of massage which uses the 'auras of the body' to pass energy from one level of our being to another, thereby enabling a better flow of energy through the 'meridians' (or channels of energy) to the 'chakras', which are considered the centres of energy.

The Centre for Oriental Medicine specialises in the practice of Hua Gong. Zhixing Wang is the practitioner and his treatment 'is part of the emergence of vibrational or energy-based medicine in the West; and it meets our collective hunger for a deeper and more subtle perception of reality'.

Just down the road, at the Lotus Centre in Dartington, eight practitioners provide a service in 'Core Process Psychotherapy' which they claim 'offers a psychospiritual approach to therapy. It acknowledges the spiritual dimension of human beings and affirms the inherent wholeness within each individual which includes all levels of being – mind, body and spirit.'

A series of 'soundshops' based in Totnes, Exeter and Plymouth were provided at £25 per session. The publicity leaflet claimed that sound has been used for thousands of years for healing by the Egyptians, Tibetans, Mayans, Incas and Aborigines. Attendance at the 'soundshop' would enable participants to recognise 'the capacity of sound to heal, to be an entrance point to another dimension and to shift energy fields'.

Meanwhile, that week the Arcturus Clinic was offering a one-day course in 'Japanese Reiki Techniques' led by Yatro, an 'Osho Neo-Reiki Master Teacher' who lives locally. Reiki energy is regarded as life energy, and it is used to heal either the practitioner or others. It is often used in conjunction with meditation, aromatherapy or crystals. The energy centres of the body are known as 'chakras', and the practitioner will often attempt to send 'reiki energy' through a problematic 'chakra'.

An increasingly popular aspect of New Age activity, therefore, is 'spiritual healing'. There are 8,000 healers on the official register of the National Federation of Spiritual Healers in the United Kingdom. Spiritual healing is recognised by the National Health Service, and patients can be referred to a spiritual healer by their GP, or indeed spiritual healers can be invited to visit patients in hospital. The most common form of healing which they practise is called 'contact healing'. The 'laying on of hands' which these healers practise is not about drawing power from an outside source such as the Holy Spirit. They see touch as a way of transferring vital energy to the patient, enabling the body's natural healing system to work.

The healer places his hands either directly on, or just above, the patient's body. The hands are usually placed on the head or shoulders, and sometimes they move their hands down the spine. Some believe that they can diagnose illnesses with their hands. They are looking for areas of the body where energy levels have diminished because of illness. Where the healer senses this kind of imbalance he will attempt to restore lost energy by passing life force through the hands. Patients often claim to feel heat passing through them when this happens.

Perhaps the most common practice is reflexology; a technique of diagnosis and treatment in which certain areas of the body, particularly the feet, are massaged to alleviate pain. This practice also emanated from China.

I was overwhelmed by the range of other healing methods on offer in Totnes. I learnt that chiropractice and osteopathy, now very much in the mainstream of health practice, can also have a spiritual aspect. The publicity explained that these healing treatments can tackle 'many deep-seated and long-standing physical and emotional problems'. Yoga and

Tai Chi are also used as healing processes, and claim to 'take us beyond the ordinary and reconnect us with our innate nature as an integral part of existence'.

Acupuncture was also very popular in Totnes, with an acupuncturist doing a brisk business in an office in the high street. This involves the use of needles on the appropriate 'meridian points' or 'energy channels' to support the body's healing processes. Practitioners claim that it can realign a disaffected and depressed spirituality.

Most New Age healers do not claim any special mystical powers, but see themselves as having an ability to tap into universal healing energy. Others use theories from different religious traditions. Dr Brenda Davies' book *Affairs of the Heart* is a good example of this. Davies is a psychiatrist and spiritual healer. This is a book for the lay market in which she introduces the reader to the spirituality on which she bases her healing practice. She freely quotes Christian sources including *The Confessions of Saint Augustine* and Dietrich Bonhoeffer's *Letters and Papers from Prison*. But her deepest spiritual convictions come from Hindu and Eastern religious beliefs. She states:

> Our capacity to move develops throughout our lives and depends to a large extent on the health and evolvement of our energy system. If we have suffered trauma which has left us feeling bitter, controlling, or unable to feel tenderness, then healthy loving becomes a minefield where games are played and people get hurt . . . Problems at one level lead to difficulties at others too, since the free flow of energy is blocked, leading to distortions up or down the system.[1]

She calls this energy system the 'chakras': 'Chakras are communication centres, wheels of light which, when in good health, are constantly spinning, drawing in the energy from the Universal Energy Field, revitalising our whole system and emitting energy, too.' Dr Davies believes that the main chakras are 'arranged in a vertical line from below the tip of the spine to above the crown of the head', and that they develop at different stages of our lives. They can be affected by different positive and negative experiences in our developmental years.

In Oriental yoga and Western magical thought these chakras are seen as 'energy centres' which absorb, transform and distribute the universal energy of *prana* or *chi*. There are considered to be seven main chakras throughout the body. *Chi*, in Chinese medical thought, is the universal energy generated by the sun and utilised within the human body. Manipulation of this energy is what helps to balance the negative/positive polarities of yin/yang. It's virtually identical to ancient Hindu philosophy.

The driving theological precept behind Davies' book, as with the teaching of many New Age medical practitioners, is that 'god is within us and therefore we, with every part of the universe, are god'. This, then, is the force that Davies and many other spiritual healers are drawing on in their practice of the laying on of hands.

Why is there such a rising tide of 'alternative' forms of medicine in a society with such a hi-tech and complex health service? John A. Lee in a scholarly paper entitled 'Social Change and Marginal Therapeutic Systems' concluded that modern medicine 'holds that illness is basically the result of mechanical failure rather than spiritual shortcoming'. He continues:

This failure is seen as precipitated by alien agents which know nothing of the patient's sins or virtues. Germs and viruses are at fault, not people. Health is a matter of nutrition, sanitation, immunization, antisepsis – not a matter of penitence and right-eousness. Material therapy is the essence of modern medicine, whether in radiation treatment, antibiotics or transplants. It is not so much that the psyche is denied, but that it is con-veniently ignored. The spirit is short-circuited by lancet or tranquillizer.[2]

In my journey towards becoming a New Age Christian I was deeply challenged by what I saw among the healers of Totnes. There was certainly more evidence of healing prac-tice in Totnes high street than I have seen in most Christian churches! But then, just after I had visited Totnes, I came across a very unusual experiment in Christian healing! On my travels overseas I was fascinated to discover that in the back room of a well-known church someone was practis-ing alternative medicine. At first my shackles rose, and I wondered if I should fill out some kind of complaint form for the denomination's head office. I discovered that this practitioner used sound and vibration as a 'healing force'.

When I mentioned this to one of the church leaders she beamed! 'I had a large swelling on my tongue,' she said, 'which was causing me great discomfort and embarrass-ment. I waited ages for an appointment at the local hospi-tal, and after some tests I was told that I would have to wait a further two months for surgery. I popped in to the practitioner at the church because I was so desperate! She used a mix of sound, vibration and prayer in the name of Jesus Christ. Within three weeks the swelling was gone. My consultant simply couldn't believe it and had to cancel my operation!'

Sadly, the ministry of healing seems to have become detached from church life in most places. There has been a growing scepticism that Christian healing has a part to play in the average Christian community.

Most of us find no difficulty in praying for someone who is about to undergo surgery, chemotherapy or some form of radiation treatment. We can accept that God works through such practices, and that his Spirit can be as active through the surgeon's knife or the pharmacist's prescription as by his direct miraculous intervention.

Why, then, can't we pray for those who are exploring some kind of alternative therapy, as long as such a course of action does not involve them dabbling in some non-Christian form of spirituality? And shouldn't we encourage Christians to take our faith into the supermarket of alternative medicine? Perhaps we could show that a mix of Jesus-centred prayer and natural treatment is a powerful force for good in times of sickness.

In some contemporary ministerial training the authority of the Bible is questioned and the miracles of Christ are refuted. This kind of outmoded teaching stems from a form of Christian existentialism which denies the supernatural as a reality. Student ministers and church leaders are taught to revere the German Lutheran theologian Rudolf Bultmann who denied the objective reality of Jesus' healings. Sadly, the influence of scholars such as this on generations of Christian ministers has largely eradicated the church's healing ministry.

It's little wonder, then, that Geddes and Grosset, in their *Guide to Natural Healing*, could say of the church:

The only form of healing accepted by many churches is so-called 'spiritual' healing. If genuine physical healing takes place, it is regarded as a problem; the Catholic church tends to distance itself from healers who claim divine inspiration in case these healers should turn out to be charlatans. While this approach is no doubt politic, it tends to undermine the place of healing in religious life. As well as this many Christians believe that the 'well of healing' dried up with the early church and limit the healing ministry of Christ to three short years of his life.[3]

Some of our leading ministers seem to show more interest in disputing the historical truth of the miracles than in recognising their potential for inspiring us to heal today. I've heard sermons in which healing miracles are inter-preted as having only a symbolic message for us, and in which contemporary healing miracles are considered to be an embarrassment!

On my journey to New Age Christianity I've become committed to the Christian healing ministry. These 'alter-native' practitioners are a powerful challenge to Christians like you and me to reconnect with the Christian healing tradition which has functioned for thousands of years, and which has always seen the connection between body, mind and spirit.

At the beginning of his public ministry Jesus announced that the kingdom of God was near (Mark 1:15) and imme-diately he began to heal the sick and to cast out demons. Some 484 verses in the four Gospels relate specifically to the healing of physical and mental illness and to the resur-rection of the dead. Jesus commissioned his 72 disciples to heal the sick and he assured them that the kingdom of God was near (Luke 10:9–10). He promised everyone who believed in him that they could perform the same miracles that he did (John 14:12). One of the signs of the believing church was that they would lay their hands on the sick and see them recover (Mark 16:16–18).

These healing miracles did not end with the Ascension, however. Peter, in the first miracle after Pentecost, gave strength to a man who was born 'lame'. Paul healed a man who had been 'lame from birth' at Lystra. When Eutychus fell from the third storey of a building in which he was sleeping and was 'taken up dead', Paul restored him to life again. Paul is credited with healing many of the people of Malta.

In his early writings St Augustine argued that healing was meant for the early church and that Christians should not look for a continuation of this practice. Later, however, in his book *Retractions* he appears to have changed his mind because of his experiences as the Bishop of Hippo (c.AD 420):

> I realized how many miracles were occurring in our own day and which were so like the miracles of old . . . how wrong it would be to allow the memory of these marvels of divine power to perish from among our people.

Thankfully, some branches of the church have kept the healing ministry of the body of Christ alive in their congregational ministry. The Assemblies of God, for example, have enshrined it in their core doctrines. In their tenth 'Fundamental Truth' they state that deliverance from sickness 'is provided for in the atonement'. They believe that, just as Christ is believed to have been sacrificed vicariously for man's sin, by taking it on himself and by relieving man of it, he is also able to take away the sickness of believers. Matthew 8:17 supports this idea, for it states that Christ 'took away our infirmities and bore our sicknesses'.

It's time for contemporary Christians to rediscover their

own ministry of healing. We need to quote James 5:14–16 to our congregations, and encourage them to do the business which rightly belongs to us!

> Is any sick among you? Let him call for the elders of the church; and let them pray over him, anointing him with oil in the name of the Lord: And the prayer of faith shall save the sick, and the Lord shall raise him up; and if he have committed sins, they shall be forgiven him. (KJV)

For too long we have practised the 'laying off' of hands. The Christian healing ministry has been discarded, or left to 'experts' in the life of the church. I have come to believe that every Christian should pray for the gift of healing, and that all of us should practise the 'laying on of hands' for the sick as part of our everyday commitment to Jesus Christ.

I'm deeply aware that I have no personal healing power, and have no 'heat-transmitting' gift or scientific understanding of human disease. I do have faith in Jesus Christ, however, and I do believe that his power is available and powerful. When I lay hands on someone in need I am doing it in his name and for his glory, representing him to a needy and broken world.

While I was writing this book, one of my friends came close to death no fewer than four times during a traumatic time in hospital. As I paced the hospital corridor in the early hours of a dark Sunday morning, I overheard two doctors discussing the prognosis. They doubted whether he would survive until morning, and I was summoned to bring his next of kin.

I have no doubt that what happened during the hours of that night was a healing miracle. I am convinced that Jesus

Christ intervened and overruled. I saw it with my own eyes and I believe it with all my heart.

On the road to becoming a New Age Christian I have decided that I will lay hands on those in need. I have no ability to guarantee the results, nor do I intend to publicise my services in a colour brochure! I am simply doing what I believe every New Age follower of Jesus should be doing – calling on the supernatural power of Jesus Christ to do good in the world and to make broken bodies, minds and spirits whole again.

NOTES

1. Dr Brenda Davies, *Affairs of the Heart*, Hodder and Stoughton 2000.
2. Quoted in Roy Wallis and Peter Morley (eds), *Marginal Medicine*, Peter Owen 1976.
3. Geddes and Grosset, *Guide to Natural Healing*, 1997.

5

Towards an Encounter with Mysticism

I am constantly staggered by the number of books about spirituality which fill the shelves of my local bookstore. One drew my attention recently, entitled *The Meditation Kit* by Tara Ward. The back cover declared, 'Learn how meditation can be deeply inspirational and help you to understand more about yourself and others.'

The book comes with a set of ten meditation cards which feature different pictures, symbols and words to aid the process of meditation. In the introduction to the art of meditation Tara gives us a step-by-step guide about attitudes, location, posture, breathing, and thinking. The author explains:

> The process of meditation also affords you the chance to take a journey (figuratively speaking) to somewhere you will probably have never been before. Many meditators have tried to explain this 'place' you go to and it always ends up being difficult to describe – for each person the experience is very personal and different.[1]

What disturbed me, of course, was that there was nothing in the book that spoke of anything remotely to do with God the Father, the Holy Spirit or the Person of Jesus Christ. You could do meditation with a candle, a word, a window or a fragrance, but you didn't need the help of any superior power. It was, to me, a journey without a destination.

Thousands of ordinary people around the UK are starting to meditate, using this or a score of other popular methodologies displayed on the bookshelves of their local bookshop. Researchers David Hay and Kay Hunt claim that 'something extraordinary seems to be happening to the spiritual life of Britain'. Their first look at the findings of the BBC's 'Soul of Britain' survey in 2000 shows that 76% of the population would admit to having had a religious experience. This was up by 59% in just over a decade and by more than 110% compared with 25 years before.[2]

One of the most well known of contemporary mystics to drift from Christianity was the movie star Shirley MacLaine. She is typical of many of today's spiritual searchers. Her quest took her to the top of the Peruvian Andes where she had a series of remarkable experiences. As a result of the water, the aroma, and the breathing exercises she found herself disengaging from her body into some higher form of existence. She wrote:

My head felt light. I physically felt a kind of tunnel open in my mind . . . I had no arms, no legs, no body, no physical form. I became the space in my mind. I felt myself flow into the space, fill it, and float off, rising out of my body until I began to soar . . . I wasn't in a dream. No, I was conscious of everything . . . it felt like a new dimension of perception, somehow, that had nothing to do with hearing or seeing or smelling or tasting or touching.[3]

So where does Christianity fit into this New Age fascination with meditation? After all, mysticism is a core part of our Christian heritage, but we seem to have buried it under a mountain of words, prayer books, OHP slides and Bible reading resources. In one of the definitive books on natural healing, *Is Britain's Soul Waking Up?*, the authors poignantly identify what has happened to contemporary Christianity:

> Modern Christianity stresses the importance of doing good deeds, loving one's neighbour and avoiding sin; the mystical side of the religion has largely been swept aside. But Christianity is essentially a mystical religion, for the true Christian seeks to be united with God through following the way of Christ, who said 'I am the way, the truth and the life. No one comes to the Father except through me.'

Over the years of my Christian nurture I was never introduced to the riches of Christian mysticism. Instead, I was schooled in what many would define as the 'evangelical quiet time'. More recently, however, I've found this kind of devotion increasingly frustrating. There's something about the culture I live in, the felt needs I have, the hunger for reality that pervades my soul, that makes five minutes of daily Bible-reading notes and a quick 'Our Father' insufficient to carry me through the stresses of the day.

I'm sure that many Christians feel the same. It's little wonder, then, that three of my friends have recently brought out CDs specifically designed to help Christians to meditate. Johnny Baker of Youth For Christ presents a refreshingly different style of music and words which many older Christians might find disturbing. Liz Babbs, whose CD *Out of the Depths* uses poems and familiar

Christian melodies, aims to help Christians to relax and focus on God. Alan Poole's *Listening to the Heart of God* uses meditations which are accompanied by the haunting sounds of Simeon Wood's panpipes. Lots of Christians are turning to resources like these as aids for a deeper kind of Christian devotion.

On my pilgrimage towards becoming a New Age Christian I have discovered that meditation is at the very heart of the church's expertise. The more I studied it, the more I came to the conclusion that we've let the world steal this treasure away from us. The rather pathetic pile of meditation cards from my *Meditation Kit* seems a very poor alternative to the thousands of years of experience which the church has in its treasure store!

The writings of many of the great mystics and seers of both East and West demonstrate that Christian meditation begins with an overwhelming sense of eternity and of timelessness. In Christian mysticism we begin by being 'engulfed by the divine' rather than by a set of black and white picture cards.

We need to begin with a process which Theodore Roosevelt, one of the most powerful men in the world, used to call 'cutting down to size'. William Beebe described it in these words:

Theodore Roosevelt and I used to play a little game together. After an evening of talk, we would go out on the lawn and search the skies until we found the faint spot of light-mist beyond the lower left-hand corner of the Great Square of Pegasus. Then one or the other of us would recite: 'That is the spiral galaxy in Andromeda. It is as large as our Milky Way. It is one of a hundred million galaxies. It consists of one hundred million suns, each larger than our sun.' Then Roosevelt would grin at me and say: 'Now I think we are small enough! Let's go to bed.'[4]

In an increasingly spiritual age, in which words seem to clutter our consciousness rather than liberate it, I want to be 'cut down to size'. I want to enter into the experience of the psalmist, who in Psalm 46 wrote, 'Be still, and know that I am God' (verse 10).

The evangelists were the pacemakers of eighteenth-century Christianity; the missionaries led the way in the nineteenth century, and the martyrs have been at the forefront of Christian witness in the twentieth century. I believe that it is the Christian mystics who will be the ones with much to say to postmodern society. They will model how to live in the stillness of the presence of God, and will play a significant role in shaping the society of the twenty-first century.

M. Scott Peck is an eminent psychiatrist from Connecticut and the author of the cult best seller *The Road Less Travelled*. It's a book of self-discovery which seems to have struck a chord with millions of people seeking inner healing and a greater sense of purpose. Peck's book has sold well in both the USA and in Britain, and is prominently displayed in many health food and New Age shops around the country. He explores something of the spirituality of his Christian journey in his later work *The Different Drum*. He writes about mysticism:

Mysticism has a lot to do with mystery. Mystics acknowledge the enormity of the unknown, but rather than being frightened by it, they seek to penetrate ever deeper into it, that they may understand more – even with the realization that the more they understand, the greater the mystery will become.[5]

The current disillusionment with consumerism, materialism and the mass production of our age has driven many to
seek a richer 'inter-connectedness', and to hunger for a new
harmony with nature and the changing seasons. Essentially,
this is a hunger for God, and I share it with them.

On my journey to becoming a New Age Christian I have
determined that I want to know more of the writings of
people like Teresa of Avila. She always wrote of herself in
the third person and described her spiritual experience in
the following words: 'The essential part of her soul seemed
never to move from its dwelling place.'[6]

In a world of growing pressure and pain, I need to discover a form of Christian spirituality which does not separate me from the world, but which enables me to find the
stillness of God's presence in the thick of the action! As a
New Age Christian I want to nurture that relationship with
Christ which is at the heart of true Christian experience. I
want to give it time, and learn how to 'practise the presence of Christ'.

All of the great Christian mystics down the centuries
commend this practice as the essential starting point for
prayer. At the end of the seventeenth century Madam
Guyon wrote one of the greatest classics on prayer, called
Experiencing the Depths of Jesus Christ. It has enriched the
prayer lives of countless millions of Christians down the
years. She wrote:

Dear child of God, all your concepts of what God is really like
amount to nothing. Do not try to imagine what God is like.
Instead, simply believe in His presence. Never try to imagine
what God will do. There is no way God will ever fit into your
concepts. What then shall you do? Seek to behold Jesus Christ
by looking to Him in your inmost being, in your spirit.

Father Jim Borst observes that there are three kinds of Christian prayer. First there is vocal prayer, using a set liturgy or spontaneous words; second there is meditative prayer, centred in a mind which seeks understanding and which thinks of God; finally, there is contemplative prayer – a prayer of the heart which reaches out to God's presence. He concludes:

> Contemplative prayer is the only real prayer, in the sense that it leads beyond words and thoughts to the reality towards which words and thoughts point. In this sense, all prayer must have a contemplative quality. Now the reality we seek is spiritual reality, a reality of our own spirit, but pre-eminently the reality of the Spirit of God.[7]

If I am to be a New Age Christian I recognise that I must take seriously the need for a focused life of prayer. My life must model that prayer leads me to a richer quality of life, a more healthy perspective, and a holistic perception of myself. My aim as a New Age Christian should be to reach that quality of prayer which the fourteenth-century mystic Dame Julian of Norwich described in 'Revelations of Divine Love':

> When our Lord gives us the grace of revealing himself to our soul, we have what we desire. At that time we are not interested in praying for anything else, because all our attention is fixed on contemplating him. This is a very exalted type of prayer that cannot, in my opinion, be described, because the origin of our prayer has been united to the sight and the vision of the One to whom we pray; wondering, enjoying, venerating, fearing him with such sweetness and delight that for the duration we can only pray in the way that he inspires us.[8]

Anyone who would become a New Age Christian must demonstrate that the inner life is as important as the creeds we recite or the doctrines we squabble about.

Donald Miller of the University of Southern California spent five years studying many of the famous 'house church' movements in his state. He discovered that they were reinventing the way Christianity is experienced in America, and were able to attract thousands of people who were alienated from institutional religion. Their laid-back style of worship and their high regard for strongly personal encounters with God fitted the felt needs of contemporary Californians. They gave individuals the freedom and affirmation to make their own spiritual journeys, but the intensity of corporate worship also heightened each person's experience of God.[9]

I want to be a New Age Christian. I want to leave behind my earthly thoughts and reasoning, my daily preoccupation with the self, and discover the greatness, the reality, the glory and the presence of God. The psalmists were driven by this mystical passion for the re-awakening of God-consciousness. Their poetry gives evidence again and again of a sense of abiding communion, and of the reality of a Divine Presence not confined to time or place. They are linked to God in an enduring unity.

So today I will find a quiet location, wear casual clothing, put on some helpful music, light a candle, pick up my Bible and read:

> Yet I am always with you;
> You hold me by my right hand.
> You guide me with your counsel,
> And afterwards you will take me into glory.

Whom have I in heaven but you?
And earth has nothing I desire besides you.

(Psalm 73:23–25)

I will let the words roll around my experience, and begin to meditate on the closeness and love of God. I will practise the presence of God and allow him to take me on a journey with a destination; a journey into healing, restoring love. A journey into New Age Christian experience.

NOTES

1. Tara Ward, *The Meditation Kit*, Arcturus 2000.
2. David Hay and Kay Hunt, 'Is Britain's Soul Waking Up?', *The Tablet*, 27th June 2000.
3. Shirley MacLaine, *Out on a Limb*, Bantam 1987, p. 140.
4. William Beebe, *The Book of Naturalists*, Princeton University Press 1988.
5. M. Scott Peck, *The Different Drum*, Arrow 1990.
6. Teresa of Avila, *The Interior Castle*, Doubleday 1961, p.211.
7. Father Jim Borst, *A Method Of Contemplative Prayer*, Asian Trading Corporation 1992.
8. *The English Mystics of the Fourteenth Century*, translated by Karen Armstrong, Kyle Cathie Ltd 1991.
9. Donald E. Miller, *Reinventing American Protestantism*, University of California 1997.

6

Towards a Green Spirituality

It was a warm Sunday afternoon when I saw the eco-warriors. I was walking by the River Thames near Kingston when I spotted dozens of them hanging onto the branches of a beautiful line of trees near the riverbank. The local council had sold the neighbouring land to a developer, and they had agreed that the trees could be felled because they would obliterate the view from the executive flats about to be built there.

I stood and watched these tree-dwellers for some time. They were certainly having fun! They were calling words of encouragement from tree to tree and passing goodies to each other by a simple system of ropes and pulleys. Meanwhile, on the pathway beneath, eager eco-campaigners enlisted my signature for their petition.

The next day there were the usual violent scenes of conflict as the police moved in to move them on. Even the television reporter sounded a note of sympathy as the chainsaws roared and the tall trees were felled.

I've never forgotten it. And as I walk the same path now I always sense a sadness deep within me. The great trees

have all gone, and the exclusive apartment block over-
shadows the river. It's fronted by some scrawny young
saplings that the council has recently planted. I hope that
the new flat-dwellers enjoy their view . . . it came with a
price.

I've heard some Christians condemn eco-warriors as
deeply disruptive and violent 'enemies of the state'. They
refute their radical statements of protest as 'dangerous'.
This kind of attitude, I'm sorry to say, misses the power
and the poignancy of their message. For, if truth be known,
what is behind this movement is a deeply held form of
spirituality.

The driving force behind the New Age commitment to
ecology is an understanding of the planet as 'Earth
Mother'. To understand this teaching we must come to
terms with the writings of the biologist Professor James
Lovelock. His book *Gaia: A New Look at Life on Earth*
teaches that the life of the Earth is like a single organism,
which is constantly defining and maintaining herself in
order to survive.[1]

Lovelock believed that the planet is not just earth, rock
and water, but that it's a self-regulating and knowing
being, and that it's connected to humanity. The Greek
name for the Earth Mother was Gaia, so Lovelock gave
the 'Earth being' this name. The feminising of Earth was
evidently a very powerful symbol in a society with
waning male influence. Teresa Moorey defines Gaia as a
goddess:

But she is not anthropomorphised. Worshippers sense that
some places are particularly 'charged' with this aura. Many
believe that the whole universe is also 'conscious' and that 'all
is alive'.[2]

Many New Agers sense the 'aura' of Gaia all around them. They recognise that there are certain centres of this power called 'Earth chakras'. It's little wonder, then, that if you believe the Earth is a living being, a being with which you are intimately connected, a being with a life of its own and suffused with divine power, you would venerate, protect and honour her.

This kind of thinking leads to a life of worship and celebration based around the goddess Gaia. It also leads to a fierce spirit of protection of her interests. Teresa Moorey sums up the consequences for a true New Age ecologist in the following way:

> The material world has been demonised and degraded by systems that look upwards and beyond for transcendence and equate the spiritual solely with the non-material. Pagans seek to venerate the earth, not merely by ritual, celebration or even mystical experience, but also in a practical sense, by looking after her . . . Unless we revere the earth and approach her with humility, as goddess at least in some fashion, we will find it well-nigh impossible to leave behind our arrogant belief that exploitation is justified because the intellect of humankind will triumph over nature.[3]

John Drane, in his provocative book *What Is the New Age Still Saying to the Church?*, quotes a New Age leader as saying:

> The Judaeo-Christian ethic is that man is the lord of creation, and can do as he wishes. The archaic-revival point of view is biological, ecological, and stresses co-adaptive relations. We are in a global suicidal crisis – and Christianity has a lot to answer for.[4]

This thinking stems from the famous thesis of John White. He argued that our current ecological ills stem from the misuse of science and technology. He concluded that this could only be explained 'as a realisation of the Christian dogma of man's transcendence of, and rightful mastery over, nature'.

To believe that Christian teaching has been the cause of ecological doom is a simplistic view, to say the least. For a start, there are countless millions of people of all religions who are partly to blame for the ecological mess that the world is in. But throughout modern history Christian leaders have warned about our stewardship of the planet and expounded our sense of responsibility to God for the way that we interact with nature.

In 1554, for example, John Calvin wrote:

> The custody of the garden was given in charge to Adam, to show that we possess the things that God has committed to our hands, on the condition, that being content with a frugal and moderate use of them, we should take care of what shall remain.[5]

The axis of the conflict between what Christians understand about the Earth and what New Agers perceive, is a philosophical problem. Christians worship a God who is beyond nature; New Agers revere a goddess who is fundamentally of nature. The gnostic Richard Smoley sums up the dilemma:

> There is a danger, I believe, in equating God with nature . . . man is not fundamentally of nature. The truest, deepest part of him is beyond the cycle of reproduction and survival. To deify nature is to forget this and to put man at the mercy of this cycle rather than to help him transcend it.[6]

On my journey towards becoming a New Age Christian I have had to revisit my theology of creation. I have come again to recognise my God as Creator. I have accepted again that the creation narratives in Genesis stress the goodness of all things created, including the Earth and especially the Garden of Eden.

I have accepted again the psalmist's assertion that 'the Earth is the Lord's'; that it is full of God's riches, his mercy, his goodness and his glory. I have rejoiced in the words of Psalm 19: 'The heavens declare the glory of God; the skies proclaim the work of his hands. Day after day they pour forth speech; night after night they display knowledge' (Psalm 19:1–2).

I have come fresh to the teaching of the psalmists and the prophets that the sustenance of the world is down to the work of its transcendent Creator. I have revisited the recurring biblical theme that God is constantly involved with his creation. I have acknowledged in a new way that God has given human beings the stewardship of the planet. In the book I co-wrote with Dr David Wilkinson we said:

Stewardship is a responsibility for which we will be judged. The sin of environmental damage is just as serious as adultery. The churches must take the lead in acknowledging the environmental sin. Perhaps in liturgies and in regular prayer, a part of confession always needs to be the way we have not tended God's garden, or thought it important enough even to think about.[7]

It is our stewardship of the planet which will one day be judged, and which God is watching . . . even now. I concur with what scientist Colin A. Russell wrote:

> By demonstrating genuine environmental concern as part of its ministry the church may yet fulfil the age-old prophetic word to 'prepare the way of the Lord'. No steward ever worked harder than when he knew his master was on his way.[8]

I also believe that God is redeeming the planet, and that at the end of time there will be a 'new heaven and a new earth'. John wrote in Revelation 21:

> And I heard a loud voice from the throne saying, 'Now the dwelling of God is with men, and he will live with them. They will be his people, and God himself will be with them and be their God. He will wipe away every tear from their eyes. There will be no more death or mourning or crying or pain, for the old order of things has passed away.'

At the beginning of my journey towards becoming a New Age Christian I took a three-month sabbatical. It was the first I've ever taken in my ministry, and it was certainly a rich time for me. It all began with a week in Swansea, visiting my son who was at university there, and a walk on the Gower. I had a commission to write a novel called *Hopes and Dreams* in twelve weeks, and as Andy and I walked over the Gower Peninsular, one of the most beautiful coastlines in Europe, I felt that I wanted to set the book there.

I decided to write about a community of New Agers, and I wanted to understand something of Celtic Christianity. And so my days were spent in three locations: a dark cavernous store which held books on Celtic

Christianity; the spectacular coastal walks of the Gower; and a small room in a terraced house near Swansea pounding out the story on my temperamental laptop!

What I came to discover was that the Celtic pagan culture had many parallels to New Age thinking. They worshipped the gods in the streams, the trees and the storms. They experienced a powerful connection to the elements and to Mother Earth. They placated the forces of nature with strange ceremonies and rituals. The sense of connection to the powers of Earth which many New Agers talk about today was very prevalent in Celtic pagan thinking.

The more I read about Celtic paganism the more fascinated I became. I felt in my bones that there is a sense in which my God is also closely connected to the planet. Then, when I came to wrestle with the thinking of the Celtic Christians, I found it deeply challenging. Instead of pointing their pagan neighbours to a 'Creator God out there', they taught of a God who infuses the planet with his life and being.

One of the greatest contributions of the Celts to the richness of Christian spirituality was their recognition of Christ in the whole of life. They understood that Christ is not only over all, but that he is in all. His presence suffuses the whole of creation and fills every creative aspect of it.

St Patrick's great prayer recognises throughout that connection to the Lord is not only in spiritual devotion, but through every aspect of our lives and even through creation itself. He wrote:

> I bind myself today to the virtue of Heaven,
> In light of sun,
> In brightness of snow,
> In splendour of fire,

> In speed of lightning,
> In swiftness of wind,
> In depth of sea,
> In stability of earth,
> In compactness of rock.

This is no heresy; it's very much what St Paul taught in Colossians – that Jesus is sustaining everything, always and constantly:

> By him all things were created, things in heaven and on earth, visible and invisible, whether thrones or powers or rulers or authorities, all things were created by him and for him. He is before all things, and in him all things hold together. (Colossians 1:16–17)

Colin A. Russell concluded:

> Through Christ, God so identifies with the suffering of Earth that one can legitimately speak of God's suffering with Creation . . . Here is mystery indeed, but here too hope for an Earth in which hope has almost died.[9]

Christians differ over how much God suffers with his creation, if at all, but Paul certainly held that creation itself was 'groaning' in a kind of birth travail that was somehow linked to God's great plan of salvation:

> We know that the whole creation has been groaning as in the pains of childbirth right up to the present time. Not only so, but we ourselves, who have the firstfruits of the Spirit, groan inwardly as we wait eagerly for our adoption as sons, the redemption of our bodies. (Romans 8:22–23)

This, then, is my green spirituality. I have rediscovered what our Celtic Christian forefathers taught: namely that Christ is immanent in all things, and that his life suffuses the planet. I am developing a kind of spirituality that recognises that Jesus is not only 'out there' but present in every tree and every flower and every sunset, and this view of Jesus is changing my view of the planet. I'm starting to see it as sacred too.

I cannot become a New Age worshipper of Gaia, but I can be a New Age Christian. I cannot revere each blade of grass I walk on as an expression of Gaia's loveliness, but I can see the power of Christ at work in creation.

On my journey towards New Age Christianity I came across an old poem that has really helped me to discover the immanence of Jesus in creation. For me, it's the starting point for a genuinely green spirituality:

> I see his blood upon the rose
> And in the stars the glory of his eyes,
> His body gleams amid eternal snows,
> His tears fall from the skies.
>
> I see his face in every flower,
> The thunder and singing of the birds
> Are but his voice – and carven by his power
> Rocks are his written words.
>
> All pathways by his feet are worn,
> His strong heart stirs the ever beating sea,
> His crown of thorns is twined in every thorn,
> His cross is every tree.

Joseph Mary Plunkett (1887–1916)

NOTES

1. James Lovelock, *Gaia: A New Look at Life on Earth*, Oxford University Press 1979.
2. Teresa Moorey, *Earth Mysteries: A Beginner's Guide*, Hodder and Stoughton 1998.
3. *Ibid.*
4. John Drane, *What Is the New Age Still Saying to the Church?*, Marshall Pickering 1991, p. 147.
5. J. Calvin, *Commentary of Genesis*, 1554, Banner of Truth Trust 1965, p. 125.
6. Richard Smoley, 'Fundamental difference', *Gnosis* 14 (Winter 1990), pp. 50–51.
7. R. Frost and D. Wilkinson, *A New Start*, Hodder and Stoughton 1999, p. 37.
8. Colin A. Russell, *The Earth, Humanity and God*, UCL Press 1994.
9. *Ibid.*

7

Towards a Sense of the Supernatural

As I write, the view from my window reveals the broad rugged sweep of Dartmoor up to Hay Tor. Even on a mid-summer's day like today the low cloud and mist are swirling across the desolate moorland in the distance, giving it an aura of mystery.

On my treks across this beautiful stretch of unspoilt moor I've sometimes been overwhelmed by the sense of 'otherness' which pervades its rugged contours. My wife and I have begun to explore this strange country, and have become intrigued by its myth and history.

Rippon Tor is a frontier hill. It's only 1,500 feet above sea level, so it's not by any means one of the highest tors. But there are tremendous views of the countryside around, including the South Hams and the sea.

On the summit of Rippon Tor are three immense cairns of stones. Just standing beside them gives me a sense of wonder and awe. Apparently, they are relics of Bronze Age times when the dead were buried under cairns such as these. Occasionally, you come across other walkers on these isolated pathways, but not all of them are simply

69

rambling from one country pub to another. Sometimes, at places like Rippon Tor, I've seen people sitting in silence with a seemingly more religious intent.

Undoubtedly, some of the folk who meditate in places like this are New Agers. One of the growing New Age activities is the ancient spiritual practice of shamanism. The shaman believes that everything is alive, and that it's all connected together in a kind of cosmic web. He sees divinity everywhere. Shaman cultures all over the world focus on the idea that the spirit can travel in transcendent flight. The ancient shaman was often regarded as a kind of king, and his rod or wand (talking stick) evolved into the sovereign's sceptre.[1]

Many today link shamanism with ley lines, a kind of force field which covers the earth. The Kogi tribe in Columbia, who have a living shaman tradition, have constructed straight paths in their land along which their transcendental flight can take place. Some archaeologists believe that shamans once created straight lines across the landscape as an outward expression of an inner experience. Paul Devereux, a major exponent of this theory, believes that these landscape lines or leys are traces of power. They are variously evolved features that have their origins in 'the ecsomatic experience at the heart of shamanism'. He believes that ancient places like Rippon Tor may have become, conceptually, lines of power. He concludes:

> They may have become physical traces, ritual pathways, avenues of the dead or whatever, but they are in essence simply traces of an effect of the human central nervous system transferred to the land.[2]

The ley system consists of a series of markers. A diverse

range of features, some of them natural landmarks, are used to mark leys. Places identified as sites of ley-line markers include hilltops, where beacons were lit on fire festival days. In addition, hundreds of mounds and cairns, standing stones, old trees, ponds and other buildings such as castles are identified as ley markers. Sometimes churches are also included where there is evidence that they were built on ancient pagan sites of worship. Other markers include old tracks, notches on hills and parallel banks known as cursuses.

Thousands of people each year trek across some of the wildest pieces of our national landscape following ley lines. St Michael's line, for instance, runs from St Michael's Mount off the Cornish coast through Glastonbury and Avebury to the North Sea near Lowestoft. There are countless other lines in the United Kingdom, Australia, North America, Chile, Bolivia, Peru and Columbia.

Although some treat this kind of walk as simply an excuse for a picnic or a mystery hunt for likely ley markers, others use it sincerely as a pathway to the transcendent and to open themselves to a oneness with the land.

What particularly fascinates me about Rippon Tor, which I believe is used by New Age shamans, is what lies on the greensward on the northern side of the tor. Just beneath the summit there is a granite cross, cut in relief on the surface of the rock. The cross measures six feet eight inches in length and about twenty-seven inches across the arms. It is evidently very ancient. Spencer Crossing, writing in 1887, quotes a previous expert Spence Bate as saying that the cross was cut to protect the local medieval community from the evil forces which they believed occupied the site.[3]

The sense of good power and evil power occupying the

land is nothing new. It's understandable, therefore, that with a new interest in ley lines there has also been a new range of Christian activity focusing on 'territorial spirits'.

While those interested in ley lines have been trekking across the landscape with map and compass, Christian groups have been drawing up 'spiritual maps' of the same areas. Many of these Christian prayer groups have begun to use a mix of historical and sociological research together with prophetic revelation to gain an understanding of what is happening spiritually in an area. Many believe that territorial spirits in such places can influence a local population.

Several years ago when I was in Northern Ireland I heard an intriguing lecture by a leading member of the Lydia prayer movement. Her thesis was that the most violent atrocities carried out during the troubles stemmed from the activity of territorial spirits. Her maps, historic documents and testimony made compelling listening. While I could accept that there may be some truth in her thesis, I'd find it difficult to blame all of the troubles on such a simplistic view of the political scene.

Peter Wagner, one of the leading exponents of this kind of ministry, believes in 'strategic level spiritual warfare'. He defines this as an occasion when Christians come to pray against high-level principalities which are active over cities, regions, nations and people groups. These powers must always be confronted in the name of Jesus.[4]

Some Christian groups believe they have been called by God to 'cleanse the land' and to 'nullify the effects of the ley lines'. Some even go so far as to draw ley lines on their maps as a means of plotting 'demonic corridors of power'. They go to 'high places' where they believe there was former demonic activity and deal with the spirits there. They watch where the ley lines run and seek to break the lines of occult power emanating from a distant pagan past.

This can be a powerful activity as long as it is seen as just one aspect of spiritual warfare. John Wimber once said that if you saw someone setting up an ironing board, then lay a shirt on it, put the iron on the shirt and say to the shirt, 'I iron you, shirt,' without actually taking hold of the iron and using it, you would think they were mad! Wimber stressed that you can only iron the shirt by doing the action! Similarly, he concluded, we need to do kingdom things like preaching the gospel, serving the marginalised and healing the sick, as well as praying that an area won't be dominated by evil powers.

David Devenish in his popular book *Demolishing Strongholds* pleads for caution in this whole activity. He points out that we can easily get caught up in the very practices we're supposed to be opposing. He is concerned that these activities can take our focus from incarnational Christian mission, which is the true biblical model. Even he admits, however, that

> there may be distinctive factors in each place that keep people from responding to the gospel. To research this could bring positive benefit. Our ministry is to pray, to preach the gospel; but also to recognise particular characteristics of spiritual oppression in particular areas and to cast out demons.[5]

In my desire to become a New Age Christian I cannot support shamanism, but I do believe that I need to rediscover something of the supernatural in my everyday life. On my journey to New Age Christianity, therefore, I have found myself drawn towards a number of projects which have a resonance with this 'spiritual mapping'.

Several years ago I joined a prayer pilgrimage for a day in the Midlands. A group of Christian leaders were walking the length of the land to pray for Britain. I found myself in a lay-by on the A1 in the pouring rain, huddled together under umbrellas with a whole network of national Christian leaders. We prayed for the towns and communities on either side of that deafeningly busy road.

I have supported this same group as they have gone on to walk through many of the most trouble-torn areas of the world, to pray for peace and reconciliation and the releasing of whatever territorial spirits might be at work. Their most publicised activity in recent years has been to walk the ancient pathways of the Crusades, all the way from London to Jerusalem. They have prayed for forgiveness for violent deeds done in the name of Christ and apologised to many Muslim congregations along the way. They have testified to a great sense of God's blessing on the project, and have been welcomed by many national leaders, as well as thousands of ordinary Muslim worshippers, in their attempt to 'cleanse' the land of its bloodstained history.

I am convinced that New Age Christians must be willing to move out of their chapels and churches and to take their spirituality into the big wide world. Over recent years my greatest moments with God have undoubtedly been outside in rural settings rather than in packed churches. There is a great deal of mystery about ley lines and ancient tracks, but one thing is for sure – the power of Christ is greater than anything in this world . . . or the next!

Several years ago I led a series of pilgrimages around the country. In all, more than 20,000 people joined us on these 'prayer walks' to ancient places. It was one of the most powerful and spiritually renewing experiences of my life. I will never forget it. Some days there were ethnic groups and middle-class white suburbanites, unemployed blue collar workers and city stockbrokers, teenagers and grandparents, and whole families, helping each other along the country trail towards their local cathedral.

A pilgrimage still throws together different kinds of people and breaks down the social barriers between them. Bamber Gascoigne, reviewing medieval pilgrimages, observed that a party of pilgrims would set out with just as much excitement as a package tour today, and they would have been just as varied a group of people.[6] A strong sense of community develops on a pilgrimage and people support one another along the way. A pilgrim group often seems like an extended family, and if there are children present it's sometimes difficult to work out who they belong to!

A pilgrimage can be a wonderful opportunity for walking in the footsteps of the great men and women of faith of previous generations. We can learn much from them, and their devotion can spur us on to greater commitment to Christ. One such pilgrimage begins on the Berkshire Downs and follows in the footsteps of Birinus, the missionary of Wessex. The pilgrims pause by the River Thames to remember how Birinus baptised the Saxon king – a turning point in the life of the church. As they pause there, the pilgrims thank God for the past and seek a fresh vision for the future.

Every Easter Monday hundreds of people make a pilgrimage to Canterbury Cathedral in the footsteps of Augustine, the early Christian missionary whose monks evangelised England from AD 597. I once joined this pilgrimage, and when we arrived at Canterbury Cathedral we all lifted up candles and passed the flame from candle to candle until they were all alight. I found it a poignant reminder that the light of Christ has been passed on down the centuries to us today.

Pilgrimages often have a prophetic role and give us a heightened awareness of the world's needs. Pilgrimage is not an escape from reality, but an opportunity to face up to the needs within us and in the world around us. The brothers of the monastic community of Taizé in France have organised many pilgrimages around the world. These pilgrimages often have a prophetic edge to them. During their visit to London the Taizé pilgrims divided into groups to pray for the city.

I remember one group visiting an area of great racial tension. I found it deeply moving to see them praying round the area in the pouring rain. They prayed in a multiplicity of languages but they knew the unity of the Spirit. Their presence in the area was a poignant symbol of the power of Christ to unite those from different races and cultures.

Pilgrimage is ideal for families, and a good occasion for new people to come and experience Christian fellowship. I've found that the ideal pilgrim group is about 20 people, and the ideal length is about five miles. Each group should have its own 'spiritual director'. If there are any children in the group there should be a leader designated to care for them and to develop activities along the walk which they can enjoy. The aim of the pilgrimage is to enrich the devotional life of each participant. Simple devotional activities are devised to involve the group as they walk along towards their destination.

As a New Age Christian I yearn to see congregations moving out of their buildings, walking together on pilgrimages to 'reclaim the land' and to connect with the ancient journeys of our Christian forebears. On one occasion I remember the whole executive of Easter People clambered up the steep path of the Great Orme on a chilly Saturday morning. We looked down on the community of Llandudno beneath and interceded for it, asking God to expel whatever evil forces might be at work there.

More recently my son Andrew and I organised a series of prayer pilgrimages across Dartmoor. As we began to plan for the week of prayer involving 30 people from all over the country, we began to discover that there are scores of crosses that stretch across the moor where the ancient pathways intersect.

Harry Starkey, in his book *Dartmoor Crosses*, observed:

> It should be remembered that there were still standing along its many paths and tracks numerous upright stones, relics of the prehistoric people who once lived upon the Moor. Many of these stones had doubtless been used as waymarks by many generations of Devonians. When the new religion swept across the country it was easy, and politic, for the old stones to be re-shaped into the likeness of the cross.[7]

As I walked along some of these ancient paths with the pilgrimage group I found the experience deeply renewing. There was something very special about walking along tracks in the footsteps of prayer pilgrims who had travelled that way centuries before. It was very powerful to stop by those ancient granite crosses and to claim the great promises of God for us in our generation.

All these experiences have given me a greater hunger for the supernatural. I suppose that this is what makes me a New Age Christian.

NOTES

1. Teresa Moorey, *Earth Mysteries: A Beginner's Guide*, Headline (Hodder and Stoughton) 1999.
2. Paul Devereux, *Shamanism and the Mystery Lines*, Foulsham 2000.
3. *The Ancient Crosses of Dartmoor*, C. E. Matthews, London, and J. G. Cummings, Exeter.
4. C. Peter Wagner, *Confronting the Powers*, Regal 1996.
5. David Devenish, *Demolishing Strongholds*, Word 2000, p. 59.
6. Bamber Gascoigne, *The Christians*, Jonathan Cape 1986.
7. F. H. Starkey, *Dartmoor Crosses and Some Ancient Tracks*, Starkey 1989.

8

Towards a New Understanding of Myself

When I was reading the Devon magazine *Connect* recently, my eye was drawn to the personal section in the small ads column. The array of different therapies on offer to the people of Devon was bewildering!

Jane Barclay was offering 'group and individual work on identity, control and choice'. Drew and Glenys were advertising 'Spirit Guidance Counselling' to help people with 'marriage, relationship, bereavement and other personal crises'. Barbara Jeffries welcomed those who were 'unhappy, alone, stressed or in emotional turmoil' to explore some integrative psychotherapy. Meanwhile Alison Tilley was offering a 'women's therapy group' using Gestalt psychotherapy, and Sally Cunis was advertising humanistic counselling for 'personal and spiritual development'.[1]

Perhaps the people of Devon are in a particularly desperate state – or is it, as I imagine, that this kind of therapy is on offer in most of the towns and cities of the UK?

Human beings like you and me are complex creatures, and many of us face difficult issues within ourselves which can stunt our development and which send us limping uncertainly into the future. John Habgood summed up the feelings of many when he wrote:

> We are often enigmas to ourselves and to each other, divided creatures with huge aspirations and capable of extraordinary wickedness. We reach for the stars, but find it hard to express what lies closest to our hearts.[2]

The self-discovery movement has sprung up to help us express 'what lies closest to our hearts'. We have become fascinated by the connection between our emotional well-being and our health. Many of us have been persuaded that the resolution of our inner conflicts is the key to personal fulfilment. The psychiatrist R. D. Laing blames this rising sense of inner turmoil on a society that has been ambivalent towards our personal inner hunger and which has often denied the spiritual needs on which 'artists and mystics throughout history have been shipwrecked'.

At the same time lots of us have become less sure of the effectiveness of psychiatry, questioning whether it is the best method for resolving our problems. Psychiatrists are qualified doctors, usually attached to a hospital, and their patients are generally referred to them by a GP. They have a diverse range of treatments available to them, including forms of counselling, group work, drug prescription and electric shock therapy. Yet each year many of us facing inner confusion prefer to look elsewhere for help.

According to Marilyn Ferguson in *The Aquarian Conspiracy*, the tranquillising drugs often prescribed by psychiatrists enabled huge numbers of previously hospitalised patients to function again in the world, but this drug therapy 'did little for the inner dissonance that helped trigger psychosis'. Laing admits that 'psychiatry means, literally, "doctoring the soul". It is unlikely that great doses of tranquillising drugs can heal a fractured soul; rather, they interrupt the pattern of distress and conflict by altering the brain's disturbed chemistry.'[3]

It's little wonder, then, that so many of us with emotional, psychological and spiritual needs have looked elsewhere for help. Disillusioned with quick-fix prescriptions of anti-depressants and mood-altering drugs we have turned to psychoanalysis and psychotherapy for comfort. We want help in our search for emotional balance, good mental health, personal development and spiritual fulfilment.

Many writers have connected with this growing hunger for wholeness. The burgeoning self-help bookshelves in high street bookshops illustrate just how popular this movement has become. A vast army of counsellors and therapists has been raised up to service this industry – another indication of New Age influence on contemporary culture.

Most counsellors use the basic principles of psychoanalysis or psychotherapy with their clients. Both disciplines tap into the subconscious of the individual, releasing hidden fears and unblocking repressed emotions. Both seek to help people to learn more about themselves. In psychoanalysis the client understands himself and his situation more clearly so that he can learn how to cope more effectively with life. In psychotherapy, however, the patient can learn to come to terms with the past, and to discover how it has affected the present.[4]

In the past the role of the counsellor was that of an aloof analyst. The client's love for the therapist was labelled 'transference', and any feelings that the therapist had for the patient 'countertransference'. The implication was that these feelings were unprofessional, and to be scrupulously avoided.

Many New Age counsellors take a more free and easy attitude to professional relationships. M. Scott Peck, whose book *The Road Less Travelled* is on prominent display in most New Age shops, is a psychiatrist and a psychotherapist. He describes this new kind of relationship:

> It is the willingness of the therapist to extend himself or herself for the purpose of nurturing the patient's growth – willingness to go out on a limb, to truly involve oneself at an emotional level in the relationship, to actually struggle with the patient and with oneself. In short, the essential ingredient of successful deep and meaningful psychotherapy is love.[5]

The New Age therapist shares his client's emotional journey of self-discovery. Many direct their clients towards the dormant healing potential within themselves and encourage their clients to explore forms of spirituality which may awaken their 'higher self'. This ministry used to be the work of ministers, vicars and priests, who have filled the role of confessor and counsellor to generations of needy people seeking greater fulfilment. They called on the power of prayer and the promises of Christ to support their flock, and didn't have much faith in Freudian psychology.

There is much debate as to whether Christians should be counselled by non-Christian therapists. Alastair Ross, Director of the Bridge Pastoral Foundation, argues: 'The faith element can prevent problems being seen clearly. The client and counsellor are tempted to collude. The Christian language can mask what is actually going on.'[6]

Richard Goodwin, Executive Editor of *The Christian*

Counsellor, disputes this. He argues: 'Secular counselling is limited. It can patch people up – but where does God come in?' Even M. Scott Peck warns of the inherent dangers of falling into the hands of those counsellors who may not take our faith seriously:

> Because psychotherapists generally belong to a sceptical if not strictly Freudian tradition, there is a tendency for them to consider any passionate belief in God to be pathological. Upon occasion this tendency may go over the line into frank bias and prejudice.[7]

It is imperative that Christians with the relevant aptitude and skills should fulfil the vocation of therapist. We need those who can offer the best that psychotherapy has to offer, but in the wider context of God's grace.

There are now 1,800 members of the Association of Accredited Christian Counsellors. They define counselling as 'that activity which seeks to help people toward constructive change in any or every aspect of their lives through a caring relationship and within agreed boundaries'. Their faith-based approach is described as 'counselling whose assumptions, aims and methods are undergirded by Christian commitment, insight and values'.

I'm relieved that so many Christians are taking hold of this opportunity. Personal development without Christian faith cultivates an approach to life that puts self at the centre. Christianity, however, teaches that ultimate fulfilment can only be found in Christ.

I want to make it clear that I deeply respect the work of the army of counsellors, whether Christian or not, whose work is with those who are in enormous emotional pain. Their healing ministry enables patients to find level ground, and they provide a safe space where clients can come to terms with their suffering or their symptoms.

I personally do not have qualms about the use of tranquillisers and other mood-altering drugs where they are used to help psychotic patients to function normally. I do not question the excellent work done by both psychiatrists and psychotherapists with people who are facing acute episodes or occasional neuroses. Their work has saved thousands from suicide and made millions of lives far more bearable.

My concern lies with the growth of psychotherapy as a means of 'self-discovery'. For many, such courses have become the latest 'trip' in the New Age supermarket. They provide an opportunity to unreservedly indulge in a process of self-examination, self-discovery, self-realisation, self-awareness and self-help. A kind of socially acceptable selfism that has led many into forms of personal spirituality which are simply not compatible with Christian teaching.

Over recent years thousands of ordinary people have become fascinated by the connection between their emotional well-being and their health. Thousands of our peers have been persuaded that psychotherapy is the key to their personal fulfilment and to reaching their full potential as human beings.

I fear that for some people the journey of self-discovery leads to a pathetic dead-end kind of 'selfism'. A kind of personal understanding which accepts that we were created in God's image but ignores the reality that we have been corrupted by our sin. This warped perspective makes the 'self' god, and life's ultimate destination our 'full potential'.

The Bible teaches that those who fill themselves with

themselves remain empty. Those who are filled by Christ are filled with a new peace and long to please God and pour out their lives for others. They hear the challenge of Jesus:

> If anyone would come after me, he must deny himself and take up his cross and follow me. For whoever wants to save his life will lose it, but whoever loses his life for me and for the gospel will save it. (Mark 8:34–35)

Because M. Scott Peck is a Christian, he echoes some of these concerns in his sequel, *The Road Less Travelled and Beyond*. There he makes it clear that it is the emptying of self and the filling of one's life with Christ which really brings true wholeness:

> We need to retain enough of our ego – the governing part of our personality – to be a functioning container. Otherwise we would have no identity at all. Beyond that, however, the whole point of spiritual growth is to get rid of our ego sufficiently to become empty enough to be filled with God's Spirit, with our true soul.[8]

One brochure advertising a psychosynthesis clinic in Totnes is typical of the attractive and relevant way in which the New Age journey of self-discovery is sold:

> Psychosynthesis psychotherapy sees the individual as being on a personal life journey to wholeness – a journey to become more of who we are. The struggles and crises we experience along the way become signposts towards that which is trying to emerge – inviting us to let go of old beliefs about ourselves and to experience new ways of being.

When I read this, I wanted to shout out loud in that New Age shop! I wanted to say, 'That's not psychosynthesis psychotherapy . . . that's Christianity!' After 30 years of Christian ministry, I've seen it happen again and again. I've watched as Jesus has led people on a life journey to wholeness – a journey to become more of who we are. I've watched Jesus as he's worked with men and women burdened by guilt, confused by the way that life's turned out, disappointed by the actions of others, rejected in love, broken by bereavement, searching for purpose or fearful of the future. I've seen him take the lives of ordinary people and redeem them by his transforming power of love.

I am a New Age Christian, and I want the kind of experience this 'psychosynthesis' brochure is advocating for myself. I want to join 'a personal life journey to wholeness – a journey to become more of who I am'. But I'm convinced that it's Jesus Christ who leads the way to such a personal quest for meaning and fulfilment. He is the one who knows me better than I know myself. I find true wholeness when I become who he created me to be.

It is a journey that begins now, and that will continue for the rest of my life. It's about a relationship with the living Christ, who changes me and heals me. It's about a transforming friendship that will enable me to become more like him. A process that prepares me for heaven.

Jesus Christ is the one who leads me towards human development, inner wholeness, personal fulfilment, and progress on life's spiritual journey. Jesus is the one who knows me best, and it's Jesus who is leading me towards the greatest fulfilment of my personal potential. Ultimately, I can only find my full potential by becoming more like Jesus Christ. John's ancient epistle sums up the hopes for personal development of every New Age Christian:

> Dear friends, now we are children of God, and what we will be has not yet been made known. But we know that when he appears, we shall be like him, for we shall see him as he is. (1 John 3:2)

NOTES

1. *Connect* magazine, February 2001.
2. John Habgood, *Being a Person*, Hodder and Stoughton 1998, p. 297.
3. Marilyn Ferguson, *The Aquarian Conspiracy*, Paladin (Collins) 1980, p. 300.
4. *Guide to Natural Healing*, Geddes and Grosset 1997, p. 164.
5. M. Scott Peck, *The Road Less Travelled*, Arrow 1985, p. 186.
6. 'Help for the Hurting', *Christianity* magazine, May 2001.
7. M. Scott Peck, *The Road Less Travelled*, Arrow 1985, p. 239.
8. M. Scott Peck, *The Road Less Travelled and Beyond*, Rider 1999, p. 247.

9

Towards My Destiny

This week, my Taurus star-line in the local newspaper read: 'Spend as much time as you can doing things which please you, no matter how simple or unimportant they seem to others. Call the Taurus line to hear more.'

This was the astrologer's advice as I started to write this chapter! What great advice! And how relevant to me after a particularly busy week! I wonder if you've ever glanced at your horoscope in the paper and wondered if it might just have something relevant to say to you?

What's so appealing about the horoscope is that it claims to speak uniquely to my situation today. It gives me the feeling that someone, somewhere, understands precisely what I'm going through. It claims to give a bit of practical advice in a very confusing world!

I suppose that's why astrology is so much a part of the New Age scene. According to a National Opinion Poll, twice as many people read their horoscopes every week as read or hear anything from the Bible. In France there are now a staggering 40,000 professional astrologers, while in the USA there are university courses in astrology, and horoscope phone services on over 2,000 campuses.

Over recent years the 'science' of astrology has made significant inroads into the business world. Many executives have turned to astrologers to find the most propitious moment for their next business agreement, publicity campaign or social event. Some timid governments have even been known to consult an astrologer before deciding on a date for their next general election.

When I label myself 'Taurus' I'm saying that I was born when the sun passed through the portion of the Zodiac named Taurus. I'm recognising that the configuration of stars in relation to this constellation plays a significant part in my destiny.

But this theory is based on an idea which everyone knows to be completely untrue. The astrologer's calculations are based on the concept that the Earth is at the centre of the solar system. Astrophysicists would struggle to make any sense of such a thesis! I suspect that, deep down, many question the credibility of what they read. After all, it must seem improbable that any 'seer' could accurately predict what will happen in the lives of one-twelfth of the population in under 50 words!

The astrologer's advice for Princess Diana's final day on Earth carried no hint of her impending doom. It read: 'Your psychic sensitivity and intuition are heightened at this time . . . you are fired up about your ideals and can spur others to action.' The following day, as her body was flown back to Britain, her horoscope ironically predicted: 'The world of mysticism is very appealing to you now and if you have talent in this area it could be a very fruitful time for you.'

Yet it's little wonder that millions of people every day find their horoscope a real source of strength in a world of

uncertainty, rapid change and broken relationships. Our
star sign gives us something to cling on to, not something
to debate! The 'stars' are not just popular with the 'blue
collar worker' or the tabloid reader; people from all walks
of life seem swayed by an interest in the stars. Nancy
Reagan, for example, consulted astrologers for guidance
when she was First Lady in the USA and living in the
White House.

Some stargazers get drawn into a world of continuous
speculation and end up paying large sums of money for
consultations with astrologers, fortune tellers, clairvoyants,
mediums, channellers, spirit guides or Tarot readers. In so
doing, they enter a gateway into the New Age scene and
open themelves to occult influences.

There are two basic kinds of astrology: 'mathematical'
astrologers limit themselves to what can be deduced math-
ematically from the client's birthdate in relation to their
astrological charts; 'mantic' astrologers, however, are
soothsayers who interpret their star chart with a fair
degree of freedom. They play by hunches and give advice
by intuition.[1]

New Agers engage in a diverse range of mantic astrology including chiromancy, crystallomancy, demonomancy,
hydromancy, lithomancy, oneiromancy, sciomancy, palm-
istry, crystal gazing, ouija, automatic writing, pendulum
dowsing and card laying – particularly Tarot. Enter any
New Age shop or open any New Age magazine and you'll
discover a bewildering range of strange and new 'mantic'
services.

It would be wrong to assume that all astrological practice is about the future, however. The famous psychologist
Carl Jung, for example, used 'mathematical astrology' as
the basis for character assessment among his patients. His

work did not involve predictions of any kind, but was a trigger for opening up a patient's life history based on a mathematical calculation involving the exact time, date and place of the client's birth.

Mathematical forms of astrology based on Jungian theory have become very popular on the contemporary New Age scene, and particularly in the use of Tarot. I recently reviewed a range of new literature on Tarot and was amazed to discover that the cards are being used by hundreds of New Agers as a primary route for 'self-discovery'.

Christine Jette observed in *Tarot Shadow Work* that many contemporary Tarot readers are beginning to view the Tarot less as a fortune-telling device and more as a tool for introspection: 'Through the symbols of the Tarot we can explore inner realms normally hidden from view.' Meanwhile Stephen Walter Sterling's book *Tarot Awareness* claims that through the study of Tarot you can find your way back from 'the mad carnival of the outer world to the natural inner world of awareness'.

In *Sacred Circle Tarot: A Celtic Pagan Journey* Paul Mason claims that his cards

> work on a number of levels, serving not only as a tool for divination, but to facilitate meditation, personal growth and spiritual development. The sacred circle refers to the progress of the initiate from undirected energy, through dawning consciousness, to the death of the old self and the emergence of the new.

One of the most fascinating and possibly 'high risk' pieces of mission in recent years builds on this innovative use of Tarot cards. Professor John Drane, a theologian and committed Christian, has joined some of his friends in using

Tarot cards in New Age festivals and Body, Mind and Spirit fairs. John told me that he and his team have invited people to use the Tarot not as a means of knowing the future but as an aid to progress in their journey towards Christian faith. John uses the cards as a means of helping clients to face the biggest questions about life's ultimate purpose and meaning. In his book *Beyond Prediction: The Tarot and Your Spirituality* he says of the cards:

> For they direct us beyond ourselves into a world where we can begin to explore our own humanity, and where we can experience for ourselves the spiritual wisdom that the Creator intended for us to have all along.[2]

John Drane's use of Tarot in this way is very much in keeping with current New Age thinking. These New Age Christian 'missionaries' use the pictures on each Tarot card as sacred symbols to raise the big questions about life, meaning, purpose and destiny. In displaying the cards they begin a dialogue about life's pilgrimage, and it's a conversation which often ends in prayer and which can ultimately point towards faith in Jesus Christ. Professor Drane and his team conclude:

> In the end they [the cards] point well beyond anything we can see and touch, and control, to the One who is at the bottom of all things, the One whose cosmic wisdom is revealed through foolishness.[3]

The dialogue between Christians and those involved in astrological practices is nothing new. More than a hundred years before Professor Drane began his work, a scholar called Frances Rolleston, an expert in ancient classics and the history of language, became intrigued by the idea that God named the stars (Psalm 147:4). Rolleston published *Mazzaroth* in 1863 in which she traced the meanings of the names of the stars. (Her work was popularised by J. A. Seiss in 1884 and E. W. Bullinger in 1893.) She spent much of the later part of her life delving into the root meanings of the names of the stars in many ancient languages. She found that similar words in different languages expressed the same basic idea, and she came to believe that they all came from a single source: the Creator God. She traced the names of a hundred different stars and discovered that all these names told the great prophetic story of Christ's redeeming love.

Kenneth C. Fleming, in his book *God's Voice in the Stars*, points out that the stars were set in place by the Creator to illustrate the signs and the seasons (Genesis 1:14) of his great redemptive story. Thus Virgo (the seed of the woman) points to Christ the incarnate Son, Libra (the required price paid) points to Christ the Redeemer, Scorpio (the mortal conflict) to Christ the Sufferer, and Sagittarius (the final triumph) to Christ the Conqueror, and so on. He concludes:

> It is true that astrology uses the signs of the Zodiac in a corrupted form, but it is not true that astrology invented them or originated them. What astrology has done is to corrupt them and change their use from that which God originally intended.[4]

I struggle with some of the interpretations of these scholars but I am sure that the night sky says more about God's grace than about my chances for winning next week's football pools! While the stars continue to 'declare the glory of God' (Psalm 19:1) and are useful in our calendar system (Genesis 1:14), the Bible forbids us from searching the stars for detailed messages about the future. Astrology is nothing new. It has been a popular activity since Babylonian times, and right from the start, God has been warning his people of the dangers involved.

There are important warnings against getting involved in any kind of divination in Leviticus 19:26, 31; Galatians 5:20; and Revelation 9:20–21. Deuteronomy 18:10–12 reads:

Let no-one be found among you who sacrifices his son or daughter in the fire, who practises divination or sorcery, interprets omens, engages in witchcraft, or casts spells, or who is a medium or spiritist or who consults the dead. Anyone who does these things is detestable to the Lord.

Some psychologists warn that too great an involvement with astrology can have an adverse effect on mental health. If we get preoccupied with what the stars indicate we can give up control of our lives – after all there's no point in doing anything which the stars don't permit! This kind of laissez-faire attitude can lead to a retreat from personal responsibility and a failure to fulfil important commitments. A fatalistic worldview can lead to accepting our weaknesses rather than making an effort to overcome them.

Any committed Christian who turns away from Jesus Christ to seek advice or guidance from any other supernatural authority is treading on dangerous ground. Paul sensed that the Christians in Colosse were tempted to use 'divine intermediaries' in their everyday lives, and he sent them a grave warning about the consequences! He wrote:

Do not let anyone who delights in false humility and the worship of angels disqualify you from the prize. Such a person goes into great detail about what he has seen, and his unspiritual mind puffs him up with idle notions. He has lost connection with the Head. (Colossians 2:18–19)

Paul made it clear that those who accept Jesus Christ as Lord and Saviour are no longer dominated by worldly powers – and they should have nothing more to do with them! They are now connected to the 'Head', whose resources are beyond measure. If we are part of a prophetic Christian community we should have no need of astrologers![5]

Although I have discounted much of what I've learnt about the New Age view of destiny, my research has deeply challenged me. I recognise that, up to now, my Christian living has been far too focused on the here and now, and I have lost a sense of God's ultimate destiny in my life. If I am to live New Age Christianity, I must take hold of the truth that God is working his purposes out in my life and make it an integral part of my daily living. Just as the reader of the stars hungers for a sense of direction, I must come to God with that same hunger and that same openness to know his will.

We don't need fortune tellers because God has given us prophets who share God's view of the future. They are people who are called, equipped and anointed with the Holy Spirit to fulfil the role of guiding us towards tomorrow. It is not their role to tell me about my chances of winning the lottery or the likelihood of having sunshine on my holiday. They are here to protect me from spiritual danger and to guide me towards the future.

My son Andy has received two prophecies about his future. On one occasion he was given a prophetic word in a small fellowship meeting by a local Christian leader who knows him well. It related to his call, his vocation and his future ministry. Some months later he was called out of a crowd of over 800 teenagers and given the same message by a well-known Christian leader. This leader had never met him before and had no inkling who he was. This kind of specific and tailor-made message was far more personal for my son than what he could read in the stars, and it was given as something to be 'weighed' rather than something that was indisputably true. It made a profound impression on him.

On my journey to New Age Christianity I've become convinced that prophetic ministry should be an integral part of every healthy church. Sadly, it's become a much neglected ministry. Our Christian expertise on the future has been stolen from us by the astrology industry. We need to reclaim our heritage. We need an authentic, biblically tested, God-inspired view of the future! It was an integral part of normal life in the early church, and it must be redis-covered today.

In Acts we read that a prophet named Agabus came down from Judea. He went over to Paul and took away his belt. He went on to tie his own hands and feet with it and said: 'The Holy Spirit says, "In this way the Jews of Jerusalem will bind the owner of this belt and will hand him over to the Gentiles"' (Acts 21:10–11).

This was a significant God-given warning to Paul and to the early church of what was about to happen, but it was also a wonderful opportunity for Paul to declare his faith and to express his confidence in the unsurpassable grace of God. Later on in Paul's very moving letter to Timothy, we read: 'Do not neglect your gift, which was given you through a prophetic message when the body of elders laid their hands on you' (1 Timothy 4:14).

A prophet is someone who is called to enable and equip the people of God to fulfil their calling. A prophet helps ordinary Christians to advance the kingdom, to make disciples and to build the church. Those who claim to have a prophetic gift must become genuinely accountable to their local church and to its leadership. I think it's best if prophets work as part of a team and are always accountable to an acknowledged apostolic leader.

David Devenish, an expert on prophetic ministry, believes that many church leaders do not know how to release and work with the prophets. He believes that this attitude is deeply unhelpful and that it robs the church of an important ministry.[6]

But prophets aren't only called by God to give input into the lives of countless ordinary people. They are also called to speak God's word about the future to governments, national leaders and nations. These prophets aren't usually princes or politicians, millionaires or popstars. They don't appear as honoured guests on chat shows. They speak from the shadows of insignificance. If history is anything to go by, they will be considered oddballs or extremists. In every generation the prophets usually go unrecognised, though their voices are the voice of God and their deeds herald God's coming kingdom.

Postmodern prophets may be considered bad like Isaiah, or sad like Hosea, or mad like John the Baptist. They will probably feel as ill-equipped as Amos the fruitgrower, or as ill-prepared as Jeremiah the farmer. They will not seek to be successful. The great prophet against the Third Reich, Dietrich Bonhoeffer, declared shortly before he was murdered: 'The figure of the crucified invalidates all thought which takes success for its standard.'

The prophets who speak of the future may have to suffer

like Martin Luther King, shot on a motel balcony; like Nelson Mandela, rotting in a South African jail; or like Mother Teresa, tramping the hungry streets of Calcutta. Yet they will be counted among the little people whom God makes great.

The horoscope is a destructive tool, and it leads us to a kind of worldview which is false and demotivating. Whatever will be will be, not because I read it in my stars, but because God is working his purposes out. He's calling me to take my part in fulfilling his will because this is what makes life worth living!

As a New Age Christian I don't need an astrologer to show me the way. I need to look towards the living God who guides me, and to a personal commitment to living for him day by day. As a New Age Christian I've discovered I have a destiny – a destiny caught up in the purposes of Jesus Christ for me. I already know the last page of the story, and it tells me that Christ's victory is complete and that he reigns for ever!

NOTES

1. John Richards, *But Deliver Us From Evil*, Darton, Longman and Todd 1974, p. 49.
2. John Drane, Ross Clifford and Philip Johnson, *Beyond Prediction: The Tarot and Your Spirituality*, Lion 2001, p. 5.
3. *Ibid.*
4. Kenneth C. Fleming, *God's Voice in the Stars*, Loizeaux Brothers 1981.
5. James Dunn, *The Epistles to the Colossians and to Philemon*, Eerdmans 1996, p. 187.
6. David Devenish, *Demolishing Strongholds*, Word 2000, p. 264.

10

Towards a New Age Christianity

There can have been few movies in the twentieth century that have captured more of the mystique of space and eternity than Stanley Kubrick's *2001: A Space Odyssey*. Its ethereal mixture of Strauss's 'Sunrise' and spinning space stations caught the imagination of millions of science fiction buffs, and raised our awareness of the grandeur and mystery of the cosmos.

The title *2001* marked the historic moment when Bowman, the time traveller, finally broke through the great frontier of space. He moved beyond the curtain of our unknowing and confronted the mysteries of the universe.

The movie is sheer fantasy, yet it reflects our never-ending quest to find 'The Answer' to all things. NASA continues to push back the boundaries of space. We have telescopes in space which give us an ever clearer view of the vast expanses of infinity before us. We, like time traveller David Bowman, want to discover how it all works.

This scientific quest is accompanied by growing speculation about other worlds, life forms and civilisations. In some strange way, the exploration of space has become, for many, a search for answers to the origin of life itself.

When I first saw the movie *2001* I remember wondering what significance the black monolith held at the end of Bowman's epic journey. When at last he found the monolith he confronted the mystery of Eternity and found The Answer. For years I wondered what it meant.

Recently I came across a tattered copy of Arthur C. Clarke's novel *2001* in a charity shop. I quickly flicked to the final chapter to read about the monolith and discovered that it was a symbol of the spiritual. It pointed towards the fifth dimension of human experience and understanding.

> Here he was, adrift in this great river of suns, halfway between the banked fires of the galactic core and the lonely, scattered sentinel stars of the rim . . . Here, Time had not begun; not until the suns that now burned were long since dead, would light and life reshape this void . . . Then he remembered that he would never be alone, and his panic slowly ebbed.[1]

Kubrick's poetic vision of mankind's search for spiritual reality is a parable for our times. New Agers believe that they are embarked on a search for ultimate meaning, and anything, even a monolith, might be the clue to the next stage of the exploration.

New Age philosophy is based on a belief that each star age lasts for 2,000 years, and that at this time we are moving from the age of Pisces to the age of Aquarius. Many New Agers believe that the age of Pisces, which lasted for 2,000 years, is now finished. Pisces means 'fish', and the end of this era symbolises the end of the era of Christianity. The dawn of the age of Aquarius is the beginning of the age of the rainbow. They perceive that spiritual energy flows into the planet along ley lines, and the places where these lines intersect are power points. These energies are strongest when there's a full moon, and at the times of the equinoxes and solstices.

The underlying thesis of the movement is that you don't need to obey a god distinct from yourself. Instead, you can do your own thing and can connect with the divine power within. You can discover unlimited potential to transform yourself and the planet so that a 'New Age' of peace, light and love can begin. New Age influence is affecting our society on every level including cinema, psychology, education, politics, business and medicine.

New Agers see the old models of Christian theology as irrelevant. If we attempt to share our Christian experience, many will simply say, 'How lovely!', for all experience is highly respected, and – in a pluralist worldview – given equal credence. Christian language and terminology cuts little ice, for much of it has been borrowed and reinterpreted in the new context.

If we talk about a 'spiritual' life, New Agers will think that we are talking of getting in touch with our divine self rather than relating to the Trinity. If we talk of 'Christ', they imagine that we are referring to a level of consciousness which we can all attain, rather than to a title only fitting for Jesus of Nazareth. 'Atonement' refers to the idea that we are already in union with God rather than being reconciled to him through Jesus Christ.

The New Ager is loathe to discern any difference between their spiritual experience and that of the committed Christian. If we point out the differences, therefore, they are likely to become angry and may even feel threatened.

New Agers believe that this new era will be an age of service, of living in harmony, of attunement with the planet and of belonging to one another. It will be an age of groups and communities, of people living and working and learning together; an age in which the whole will be seen as greater than the sum of the parts; an age of synergy. A committed Christian who lived and worked in a New Age community for five years described the ethos of her community to me.

'A lot of the people in the community were trying to make money through craftwork, thatched roofing, basket weaving or carving. They were very skilled and intelligent people. They sold their work through craft shops. They taught each other and shared their skills. They spent a lot of time with one another. There was a great sense of community. It wasn't as if they just spent one hour together on Sunday morning. They really belonged to one another.

'Everyone was engaged in a great spiritual search. They used to talk to me about my beliefs and shared their experiences of the past. They had a lot of rituals. Lots of things were done sitting in circles where all were equal, with no one at the head or foot. They had a lot of signs and symbols. They gave everybody the opportunity to express themselves, and only one person was allowed to speak at a time. Everyone had freedom of speech. They used the colour white a lot as a symbol of purity.

'They didn't want to be preached at. They had tried churches and felt that they were "put down" in that form of religion. So we developed a caring role, sharing the gospel through our actions. We asked ourselves, "What would Jesus do?" It was not a mission of words, but a mission of actions. We wanted our deeds to speak louder than our words. When I go back to the community, the reaction is overwhelming. They say that they were seeking enlightenment and saw what they were searching for reflected in me.

'I had become a servant in every sense of the word. I was very

accessible. I became a listener. Lots of people wanted to talk about their past experiences and their journey to where they were. They often watched my reactions. A lot of them had been very hurt by Christians. We needed to demonstrate true Christianity. Our home had an open door and was always full of people.

'I bring into my Christianity now a richness of experience from living with the New Agers. Their simplicity of living is high on the list. We can so easily get caught up with materialism and "keeping up with the Joneses". There was none of that in the community – they shared everything. They were searching for spirituality. In the Christian culture we can feel that we have reached a peak. But they were constantly searching for the next experience.'

Essentially, then, the New Age movement is about a search. The New Age searcher may not find a monolith, but they hope to discover some clue as to how and why things are as they are. It is a journey about meaning, purpose and existence, and it's a journey which poses the most fundamental questions of all.

While Sabina Holt Brooke was a student at art school she got involved with magic and witchcraft and began to indulge in the form of mysticism known as Kabala. From that she moved quite easily into the hippie movement which accepted all those things, but which also embraced belief in nature spirits.

At the same time she began to get involved with drugs, which she saw as part and parcel of the hippie culture. She said, 'It was as if we were looking for other worlds, and the mysteries of lost civilisations.'

Sabina had been brought up a Catholic, but she became very anti-Christian, thinking that she could disprove the existence of Jesus. She was particularly disillusioned with

the dogmatic pre-Vatican II Catholic Church. 'I was looking for spirituality,' she said, 'searching for a way of life
that had integrity. Ultimately I was looking for God. I
believed that we were ancient reincarnated beings – gods
leading our generation into a New Age.'

Sabina went to a conference at Loch Earn with all the
major hippie leaders of her day. From there she ended up
in the Findhorn community and was the first young person to join the community of about six people in their
fifties. Sabina said:

*'I was there for about 18 months. The community there is now at
the head of the New Age movement in this country. They were
very much into nature spirits and viewed themselves as bringing
things from the spiritual realm into the material. The community
is on a power point; on ley lines connecting to other significant
places like Glastonbury and Iona on the worldwide power network.'*

Sabina really thought that she had found the answer to
her many questions in this community, but eventually she
wanted more. So, after Findhorn, she went into a hippie
community and ended up on Papa Stour, a tiny island near
Shetland.

*'I was into "Gurdgeff" at the time. It followed a system very sim-
ilar to transcendental meditation, and we were hoping to find
our "permanent eye" and discover who we really were. I was
meditating in my little hut, trying to find my permanent eye,
and I had my eyes closed (I wasn't on drugs at the time).
Suddenly, Jesus appeared to me. His presence filled the hut, and
he said, "I am the way, the truth and the life." It completely
changed my perception. I asked my neighbour, who was a lapsed*

Catholic, to call the Catholic priest. He was a dear old man, but was not interested in Jesus. Then I asked the local Church of Scotland minister to help, but he told me that he was an existentialist. I couldn't find anyone who could tell me about Jesus.'

Three months later Sabina met a Christian leader who explained the Christian gospel to her. She was told that she could have a personal relationship with Jesus and know him as her friend. He came to visit Sabina and her husband, bringing lots of Christian tracts with him. They both accepted the Lord Jesus Christ as their Saviour. They burnt all their New Age books and symbols, and very quickly the hippie community rejected them. Soon afterwards they started a Christian fellowship on the island.

What, then, did Sabina bring into Christianity from her years of experience in the New Age? Sabina told me:

'We have brought with us a desire to pursue the careful stewardship of God's creation. Above all, because I've had strong spiritual experiences in New Age spirituality, I know there is a power. It's given me discernment. So many churches don't understand spiritual power.'

My exploration of what it means to be a New Age Christian is summed up by the word 'journey'. In the early days of my Christian discipleship I was taught that I needed 'blessed assurance', that I had 'received salvation' and that I was now 'born again'. All of these truths I still accept, and they are all precious to me.

What has changed? I am now aware that, even with my blessed assurance, received salvation and born-again experiences, there is more. The New Age Christian is someone who recognises that they have not arrived – there is more.

Much more. And I believe that much of it is to be discovered in the ancient treasure store of our Christian heritage.

Dr Andrew Walker is a lecturer at King's College in London. Several years ago he exchanged a failed form of Pentecostalism for a living spirituality based in Greek Orthodox Christianity. He recognised his need for something richer than hymns, hand-clapping and hallelujahs and found it by connecting with the ancient prayers, disciplines and liturgies of a church which claims that it has the closest connection with early Christendom.

I empathise with his journey. I recognise that the spirituality of the New Age Christian must be far deeper than the shallow emotionalism that some of us have been getting by on. If Christianity is to flourish in this new era, it will need to find a new depth and richness in order to stand alongside the diverse range of spiritualities now on offer. If it doesn't deliver a raw kind of spirituality it simply won't relate to a society focused on the supernatural.

Karen Drummond Hunt was in a cult called 'the Emin', although it didn't look upon itself as a cult. It was very academic, moralistic and religious. It was a mix of different beliefs and presented itself as helpful, healing and a way to God. It claimed to make its members acceptable to God through a refining process.

'I was looking for God. In the beginning it looked as if it was light and a way of truth. There was a power associated with it. I regularly attended church until I was 19 and came to the conclusion that God wasn't in it. It seemed that people were just going through the motions. It didn't fulfil what I was looking for. I started looking at other places.

'My husband and I were both in the cult. I began to look at it and started to discover that it wasn't what it said it was. The

negative things I had noticed in church I also saw in the cult. What was said and what was done were two different things. My awkward questions were not well received. I kept questioning and questioning.

'God really did intervene. My husband was in Glasgow Central Library and felt guided towards a book. He picked it up and read it. The book was called The Way of Truth. I suppose that if we had come across it now that we have studied the Bible, we would have thought that its content was dodgy, but it was enough to get us praying and looking at Jesus.

'We had looked at Jesus in the cult, but he had been referred to as "JC". He was not presented as God and Saviour, but only as an enlightened man who had "made it". We decided to move house to Shetland. We went to look at one house and as we were being shown around it we noticed that there was a plaque on the wall saying something like "Jesus loves you", and so we asked the lady who owned the house, "Do you believe in Jesus?" She said she did and we got to know her better. We told her about our search and she was able to answer most of our questions. We discovered that a lot of what we had been told about Christianity wasn't true. We made quite a cold-blooded decision really. If we were going to follow Jesus it had to be an all or nothing decision. We decided to go for it and that was it.

'From my experiences in the New Age I bring to Christianity a deep awareness that the supernatural is real. That has to be part of what we present as Christians. Jesus is supernatural and following him is not about just going through the motions. I know that if Jesus could save my husband and me, he can save anyone. We were so far off the track at times that we know it is only through God's grace and mercy that we are saved.

'We have a real desire to see the church wake up and see what it is they've got. Nearly all the New Age people I know have been to church. That is usually the first place that their search takes *them, but often they don't find fulfilment there. I'm now a Christian. I've been rescued from New Age spirituality. It is a bondage. It's not the freedom it pretends to be. The fact that people are seeking should encourage us. They are spiritually awake. It is easier to reach them than it is to reach those caught up in materialism. They are searching.'*

Sadly, many of us have become shallow Christians whose spirituality bears no comparison to the depth of mysticism of earlier Christian traditions. If you would join me in becoming a New Age Christian, you must be willing to delve into the riches of our Christian heritage and offer the world a spiritual reality that has been tried and tested over many generations.

David Adam is the vicar of Lindisfarne. He has written extensively about Celtic spirituality and his personal attempt to interpret their disciplines for today. He believes that we need to discover the precious links between all living things; that there is a unity at the very heart of our world, and it can be experienced by each of us. He teaches that a combination of God-awareness and ecology is basic to this approach.

In the Dark Ages St Aidan held out the light of Christ to a godless and secular generation. Through his influence much of England and Europe was affected by the gospel. Yet Aidan was not based in a large city or on a busy thoroughfare. His ministry was established on the obscure island of Lindisfarne, known as Holy Island, off the Northumbrian coast.

Lindisfarne is only one and a quarter miles from the shore. It's a tidal island, which means it can only be approached by land when the tide is out. This gives a rhythm to its life. In recent years thousands of people have been making pilgrimage there to connect with this simple rhythm and to discover the heritage of the Celtic saints.

Aidan used to look out at a little boat at anchor to see whether the tide was coming in or going out. He built a discipline of spirituality on this daily flow of the tide. He taught his island community to receive the love of God as the tide came in, and then pour it out in intercession, praise and loving service to others as it went out. Aidan knew that too many lives become trivialised by too much action, and that each of us needs to be refreshed by the incoming tide of God's love.

Every day, between the tide coming in and the tide going out, there was an hour when the tide was still. Aidan taught that when the balance between our receiving and our giving is right we, like the still waters between tides, discover perfect peace.

Gradually, more and more people visited Aidan and his praying community, including the king and the royal family. Eventually, Aidan had to create another island refuge of his own in order to restore the balance between giving and receiving in his life. This tiny island was known as the 'desert in the ocean'. It was a place of great spiritual blessing but also a place to fight the powers of darkness both within and without. Aidan went there to be alone with God and to give priority to prayer. It was a wild rugged place and his prayers were often punctuated by the deafening roar of the sea.

Ray Simpson is the guardian of the community of St Aidan and St Columba on Lindisfarne. He is establishing communities of Christians around the world who want to follow the spiritual disciplines of the Celtic saints. After centuries of neglect, this aspect of Christian spirituality is being rediscovered.

Busy men and women, who are caught up in the pressures of a hi-tech materialistic society, are discovering that they need to connect with the ebb and flow of the tides of Lindisfarne. They have a new desire to take in from God and to give out in compassionate service. They want to discover the perfect rest that comes when the balance is right.

Thousands of Christians of all denominations visit Taizé, Iona and Holy Island to learn something of their spiritual heritage and tradition. If we are to make a relevant response to society's growing hunger for spirituality, we must take time to connect with our Christian heritage. We must walk these ancient paths, and relearn these ancient disciplines. We must learn again the ancient Christian disciplines of meditation. Our goal should be to reach a life of inner stillness, and to become silent and focused on God alone.

One man who has been a 'voice crying in the wilderness' in these matters for many years is David Pott, of the Fountain Gate community. David looks back to the 1960s as a watershed for him:

'I was a Christian, but called to live in the "counter-culture" scene of the time, sleeping rough in the parks. I did some research and wrote papers on counter-culture. It affected quite a lot of people and these ideas were influencing ever-widening circles of seekers. In the 1990s it all seemed to come to fruition, and we saw the shift from modernism to postmodernism. I maintained a strong Christian position while striving to be culturally sensitive. At the time I met my wife, we were both interested in Celtic Christianity and we spent some time in Iona, exploring community living.

'The vast majority of Christians today have been influenced by modernism. They are, on the whole, accommodating to

humanism and materialism, but are very scared of New Age spirituality and paganism. As Christians we need to think about how we relate to postmodernism and New Age spirituality.

'At the Fountain Gate community in London we ask the question, "How do we do this thing called church?" We try to be a "church without walls", emphasising the importance of community and exploring "new monasticism". A rhythm of prayer is important, with prayer times morning, noon and evening, reflecting the seasons in their themes. The use of liturgy is extremely significant in these prayer times, although we don't exclude spontaneous, extempore prayer. We also hold pilgrimages, and those involved in New Age spirituality can really resonate with these.

'There needs to be a more creative approach to worship in the church with a greater use of symbols. Our Ceilidhs are working quite well. We hold them about every two months in the Celtic tradition. People come together and share stories, poems, riddles and songs. A wide variety of people come – some even come with Buddhist perspectives. The evenings are challenging enough without being threatening. We also regularly hold Shabbat meals. During these meals we use slightly Jewish/slightly Celtic forms of liturgy that we have compiled ourselves. Creation and creativity are closely linked, so creativity in worship is vital.'

My research for this book has led me to meet many unusual and dynamic Christians, and my only regret is that I don't have another three volumes in which to tell all their stories!

Louise Donkin was involved with New Age spirituality at university, and was particularly concerned with the ecological movement and radical action for societal change. Since becoming a committed Christian she has brought her commitment to justice into the life of the church. Hundreds of students, Christians and non-believers, attend the conferences of 'Speak' to work for a better world. Louise is convinced that Christians must be at the forefront of change, and just as William Wilberforce fought slavery in his generation, there are many issues which should engage us today.

Louise believes that justice issues and intercessory prayer are the twin forces which demonstrate to the world that Christianity is real and credible. She writes:

> It is our firm conviction that we need to work towards seeing a whole generation raised up rather than building another organisation. Whatever our calling, a concern for justice should feature somewhere in the people we are and the actions we take. We can all act as a catalyst to encourage other people to use their voice.[2]

Even the Establishment seems open to a new look at the challenge posed by New Age spirituality. George Carey, the Archbishop of Canterbury, in his lecture entitled 'Healthy Religion' at the London School of Economics, concluded:

> I believe that at its best Anglicanism has a healthy openness to other insights, without, of course, denying its own essential convictions. Take, for example, the question of response to New Age spiritualities. I recall that many years ago when I began to read the work of Christians open to such spiritualities, such as Matthew Fox, very few were more hostile than I in criticising what I took to be syncretistic ideas at odds with mainstream Christianity. It took me some time to appreciate that the New Age emphasis on the sacredness of creation, the

interconnectedness of all God's creation and the need to be concerned for our environment, were all deeply Christian themes – but ones which had been too often neglected in the church.[3]

Many of us need to become apprentices in the spiritual life and to be guided by those who are further along the journey of prayer than ourselves. Perhaps the church needs to raise up a new generation of spiritual directors who can navigate hungry souls towards the feast of good things which God has for us.

Saint Aidan recognised that it isn't easy to develop a life of prayer and contemplation, so he set up a system of mentoring to encourage his followers to embrace these disciplines. Each of the brothers whom he personally mentored adopted an *anamchara* – a cell mate. This new member of the community would learn by rote 150 psalms, a gospel, and spiritual songs which were taught him by the senior brother. In turn the younger member would take on his own *anamchara*, and so the spiritual disciplines were passed on from one to another.[4]

This kind of spiritual mentoring is growing more popular again at the moment. Many committed Christians are discovering that they need a spiritual 'director' to help them in their journey of prayer and devotion.

Timothy Jones, in an article called 'Believer's Apprentice' in the American magazine *Christianity Today*, found that his director helped him to make sense of everyday life and to spot God's activity in the mundane. He began to get a true focus on the events of his life and gained great strength from the knowledge that his director was praying for him.

In the very helpful book *Connecting: The Mentoring*

Relationships You Need to Succeed in Life all Christians are encouraged to find a spiritual director. This director would enable believers to assess their own development in the Christian life, point out areas of strength and weakness in spirituality, and help them to take initiatives for change and growth. Above all, the spiritual director must provide accountability and give the kind of guidance that leads to spiritual maturity.[5]

If you would join me on the journey towards New Age Christianity, you must be willing to move beyond the familiar trappings of our comfortable Western church life to meet God face to face. We must seek a kind of personal spiritual renewal that will enable us to demonstrate not only that it's true, but that it works!

The author Liz Babbs has been of great help to me in my research for this book. In 1990 she was very ill and was in such pain that every part of her body was sensitive to touch. She had a rash all over her skin and was very bloated. She had terrible weakness in all her muscles. At this time she was tempted to try transcendental meditation to see if it would help, as its benefits were being much advocated in M.E. magazines. At about that time, however, a Christian gave her a booklet about Christian meditation, so she decided to give it a try. She wrote:

I was amazed because I didn't feel that I really understood fully what I was doing, and so when I started hearing voices I thought I must be going mad! But as time went on, God continued to reveal to me that he would heal me. I had no idea that meditation and contemplation was such a powerful form of prayer. The deep relaxation and quality of rest that I experienced was incredible. Somehow, I had stumbled across a means to draw close to God's heart and so commune with the divine source of all healing. My journey into contemplative prayer and meditation had resulted in me being able to hear God, and this ultimately led to my recovery from M.E. I now lead sessions in relaxation, contemplation and meditation on my M.E. retreats, so that others can experience the healing power of drawing close to God in this way.[6]

There are great blessings for all who would take Christian spirituality seriously, but there are dangers too. Perhaps we need another John Wesley to guide us into this new mission field. His theology respected the authority of the Bible. He opposed the domination of reason that his Anglican contemporaries so appreciated, and he defied the reliance on feelings so strongly advocated by revivalists. Wesley chose a middle way: an awesome respect for the Bible, but interpreted in the light of reason, church tradition and personal experience.

His evangelistic fervour and his advocacy of 'the strangely warmed heart' challenged the cold deism of the established church; but he fiercely protected his followers from the fanaticism which England had seen in the previous century.

In the same way, the church leaders of this new age must guard the flock, lest feelings become more paramount than the Bible. While the society of the new millennium may hunger for that 'spiritual feeling', it must be based on the unchanging and eternal facts of the gospel of Jesus Christ.

In essence, the road to becoming a New Age Christian is a personal one. It's about nurturing the relationship with Christ which is at the heart of all true Christian experience. We must give it time, and learn how to 'practise the presence' of Christ.

In the future there will be little interest in the cerebral

theological analysis of our believing. The question on everyone's lips will be far more pragmatic, for they will ask: 'Does it work for you?' 'Could it work for me?'

Where, then, should you start if you would become a New Age Christian? Perhaps you should start in the treasure trove of Christian mysticism. For it is this rather than theology, philosophy or apologetics that will speak most to this dawning age of Aquarius.

Philo, writing in the same era as Jesus Christ, taught that

> The Kingdom of God is within us, even in this life;
> for this life's reward is holiness, the vision of God;
> its punishment, that of being what sinners are.
> This vision or knowledge of the Most High
> is the direct personal communion of a soul
> that no longer reasons,
> but feels and knows.

Augustine taught in his spiritual classic *Confessions* that first must come purgation, then illumination, culminating in the ecstasy of union with Christ.

> What is this which shines on me and pierces my heart without hurting it? I shudder and am aflame at the same time: I shudder, because I am so dissimilar to it, and I am aflame, because I am so similar to it. It is Wisdom, Wisdom itself which shines on me, breaking up my cloudiness, which yet covers me once more as I fall away from it through the darkness and rubble of my troubles.

Many women have contributed to the richness of Christian mysticism. People like Hildegard of Bingen, Elisabeth of Schoneau, Angela of Foligno, Catherine of

Siena, Teresa of Avila, Madame Guyon, Marad Acarie and Julian of Norwich. Maybe women will lead the church again in the journey towards New Age Christianity. Angela of Foligno (c.1470–1540) once wrote:

> And when I looked, I beheld God who spake with me. But if thou seekest to know that which I beheld, I can tell thee nothing, save that I beheld a fulness and a clearness, and felt them within me so abundantly that I can in no wise describe it, nor give any likeness thereof.

I am becoming a New Age Christian, and I am not alone. Many committed Christians are looking for something deeper in their everyday life of faith. I am discovering what Jesus meant when he said: 'Because I live, you also will live. On that day you will realise that I am in my Father, and you are in me, and I am in you' (John 14:19–20).

The road winds towards the horizon ahead. It is long, narrow and difficult. It's the journey of Christian discovery – the most important journey of all. The question you may ask yourself is, are you hungry for more of God? And, if so, will you come on this journey too?

NOTES

1. Arthur C. Clarke, *2001*, Arrow Books 1968.
2. 'Speak' newsletter, Winter 2001.
3. 'Healthy Religion', lecture at the London School of Economics, 19th April 2001.
4. David Adam, *Flame in My Heart*,Triangle 1997.
5. Stanley and Clinton, *Connecting: The Mentoring Relationships You Need to Succeed in Life*, NavPress 1992.
6. Elizabeth Babbs, *Can God help M.E.?*, Eagle 1999.

When I Can't Pray

by Rob Frost

Praying isn't always easy. There is so much in life to throw us off course and keep us from developing regular communication with God.

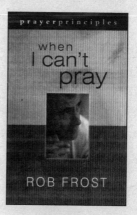

Rob Frost provides food for thought and prayer for up to four weeks of daily meditations. The result is a celebration of the most rewarding relationship we can have.

This book won't suddenly make prayer easy . . . but it might make it happen.

Kingsway Publications

A Closer Look at Science Fiction

by Anthony Thacker

Is the truth really out there?

Science fiction is one of the foremost ways in which our culture tries to explore creative possibilities and grapple with the big issues of life:

- Why do we exist?
- How do we handle our increasing power over the mechanics of life?
- What if we're not alone in the universe?
- Where does evil come from?

Anthony Thacker looks at the popular face of science fiction, and addresses the key *spiritual* and *moral* themes raised, especially by some of TV's most popular series.

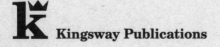 **Kingsway Publications**

A Closer Look at Harry Potter

by John Houghton

J K Rowling's *Harry Potter* series is uncontested as the greatest children's book phenomenon of all time.

Yet, while the world applauds, Christians are divided, and many are calling for the books to be banned from state schools and public libraries.

John Houghton himself is a writer of fantasy for children. In this book he offers an alternative to the secular wisdom on the conflict between good and evil. His considered critique offers timely and valuable insight for parents, teachers and all those involved in children's ministry.

This book is a must for all those who want to encourage a culturally literate, wise and godly generation who know how to have fun without regrets.

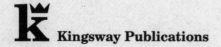 Kingsway Publications

Buying and Selling the Souls of Our Children

A Closer Look at Pokémon

by John Paul Jackson

Can you feel God's heart breaking?

Children of destiny are being enticed and lured by the spirit of the age. Some have drifted unknowingly into the realm of darkness. Will our sons and daughters accomplish their God-given mandate for this hour? Or will they become a lost generation?

'I highly recommend this book.' – Wesley Campbell

'Read! Be warned! Be equipped.' – Lou Engle

'A warning that we all need to hear.' – Jack Taylor

JOHN PAUL JACKSON is founder of Streams Ministries International. He travels extensively around the world teaching on the art of hearing God, dreams, visions and the supernatural.

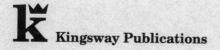

Kingsway Publications